A GUIDE TO THE INDUSTRIAL
MOLE VALLEY DIS'
BY PETER TARPLEI

CW01466893

52: Clock House Brickworks, Capel

Photo: Butterley Brick Ltd

1: INTRODUCTION

Mole Valley District was formed at the reorganisation of local government in 1974. It consists of the old Leatherhead and Dorking Urban Districts together with much of the Dorking and Horley Rural District. It covers about 100 square miles stretching from Chessington (in the London Borough of Kingston-upon-Thames) in the north to Gatwick (in West Sussex) in the south.

Extractive industries were an important part of the industrial past, the extracted materials varying as the geology changes across the District. Chalk quarrying and brickmaking were particularly important and were carried out at a number of sites in the area.

Railways and roads both use the north-south Mole Gap through the North Downs. The A24 and A25 roads cross at Dorking as do the London–Horsham and the Reading–Tonbridge railway lines.

In general the book gives brief descriptions of the main industrial activities in the District referring, where possible, to sites and buildings which are still in situ. As well as the larger industries, other sites of particular interest are described; especially items which may not be included in other types of local history guide books.

This book does not cover all industrial activities in the District, but it includes the information available at the time of its preparation. The Group would welcome details of any errors or omissions in the Guide so that our records, and those of others to whom we supply information, can be as accurate and comprehensive as possible.

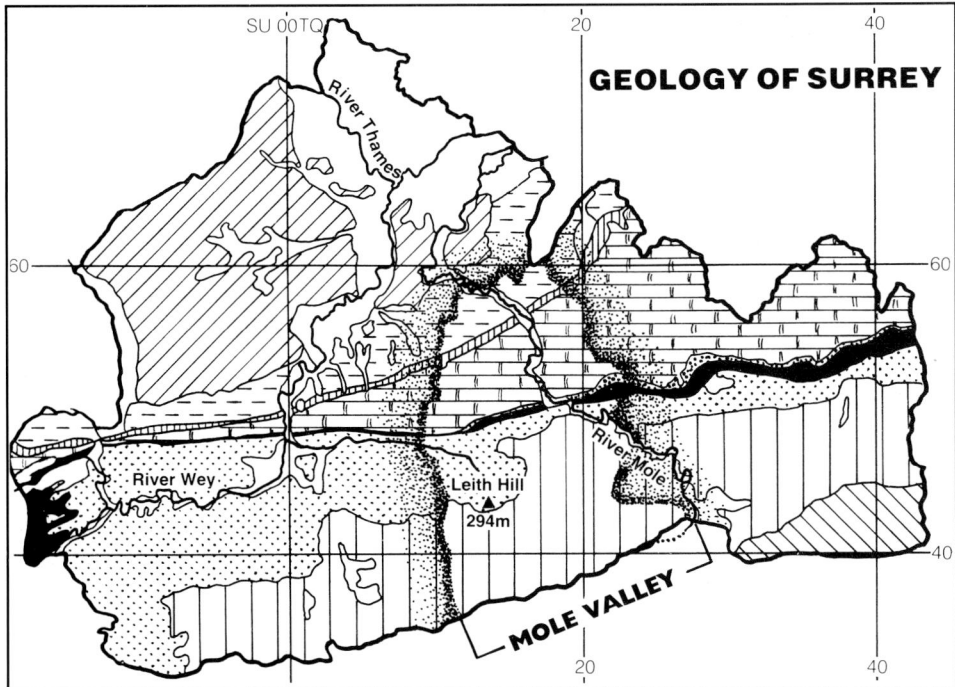

GEOLOGY OF SURREY

SU 00TQ
River Thames
River Wey
River Mole
Leith Hill
294m
MOLE VALLEY

☐ Aluvium and Valley Gravel		▨ Upper Greensand	
▨ Bagshot Series		■ Gault	
▨ London Clay		▨ Lower Greensand	
▥ Reading Beds		☐ Weald Clay	
▨ Chalk		▨ Tunbridge Wells sand	

2

20: Betchworth Limeworks and opposite (below) Betchworth from the air. Both views, c1952

Photos: SIHG Collection

From the map showing the geology of Surrey it will be seen that there is a wide range of soils encountered across the District from north to south.

In Roman times, and since, brick and tile making has taken place in the London clay in the north. Then there were potteries and brickworks in the Reading beds and chalk extraction for lime-burning, building stone and for agricultural use from the North Downs. From the Upper Greensand firestone, building stone and hearthstone for cleaning were obtained whilst brick and tile making occurred in the Gault, and sand and sandstone were quarried from the Lower Greensand.

To the south of the District lies a large area of Weald Clay from which some ironstone was mined in the past and which still supports a number of brickworks of considerable size.

Working roughly from north to south across Mole Valley we list a number of sites where extractive industries have taken, or are still taking, place; with a final section on the Wealden iron industry.

I ASHTEAD COMMON
TQ 184 601 ❖

A Roman tile works existed on the Common, and nearby there are spoil heaps considered to be from a brickmaking operation in the 17th century which produced the bricks for the wall of Ashtead Park.

Cottages at the eastern side of Newton Wood, near to which is a flooded claypit, are left from a brickworks which ceased operating during the second half of the last century. Later the complex was used by gamekeepers.

2 GREEN LANE BRICKWORKS, ASHTEAD
TQ 173 585

The brickworks in Oakhill Road/Green Lane

were owned by J L P Sanderson who bought 30 acres of land in 1896 on which he erected kilns close to the railway. However, before he had made many bricks he went bankrupt in 1898. The works were bought by M N Inman who kept on the previous owner as manager making bricks here until 1912.

In 1918 Weller's Rose Garden took over the site, landscaped the clay pit and opened it as a swimming pool. This was known as 'The Floral Pool' and continued until 1959; the flooded pit remains in the garden of 'The Floral Bungalow' in the Chase.

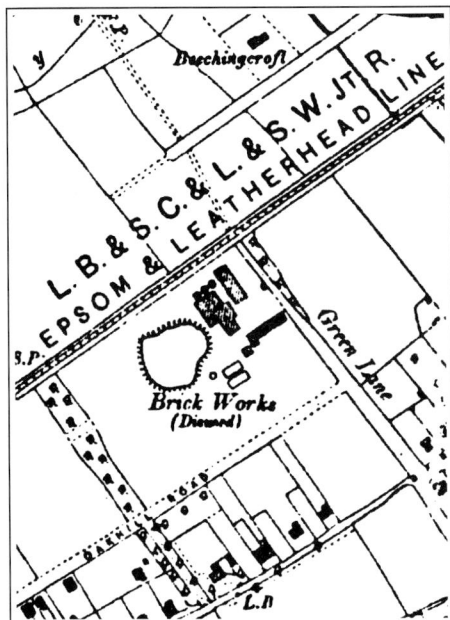

2: Green Lane Brickworks, Ashtead *OS Map, 1915*

3 CHURCH ROAD BRICKWORKS, ASHTEAD
TQ 179 584

G P Sparrow bought this site in 1880 and built a brickworks which operated until about 1909, when he sold the remainder of the site for use as a cinema and for housing.

The kiln has gone but two cottages which he built for the works, known until recent times as Brickfield Cottages, remain as numbers 216 and 218 Barnett Wood Lane.

4 WOODBRIDGE BRICKWORKS, LEATHERHEAD
TQ 160 583 ❖

This works was south of Rowhurst to the west of the footpath from the Rye Brook bridge near Tesco's stores to Teazle Woods. Evidence of clay digging may be seen in the woods; some of the pits are water-filled, and the base of a kiln is still recognisable. This brickfield was active during the latter part of the 19th century.

5 COPTHORNE BRICKWORKS
TQ 170 571

This brickfield operated during the 19th century but had ceased by 1897. It covered the area south of the allotments

6 BUCKLAND CHALK PIT
TQ 222 524 ❖

4 This chalk pit at the end of Buckland Lane at the foot of the Downs contained two or three small lime kilns but it is now very overgrown.

7 WEST HUMBLE CAVES
TQ 154 520 ■

Here there is a large medieval chalk quarry in the escarpment of the hill from where freestone chalk blocks were mined, as well as chalk for agricultural use and lime making for mortar. The mines were surveyed in 1947 and were found to extend 50 yards east to west and 30 yards north to south

The entrance was sealed in 1975 following a serious incident in which a boy had to be rescued from the 'caves', but access has been retained for bats to use the several hundred feet of underground passages.

8 STONYROCK LIMEKILN
TQ 123 518 ❖

A small chalk pit is on the north of Stonyrock Road by a right-angled bend. There are remains of the limekiln on the opposite side of the road.

9 DORKING LIMEWORKS
TQ 159 502

This works was reputed to produce some of the best lime in England for building purposes. It was used in the late 18th century in the construction of Somerset House and the Bank of England, whilst in the next century its property of hardening under water was the reason for its use in constructing the West India and London Docks.

The works closed in 1939 but parts of the site are now used as a refuse depot.

Chalkpit Terrace and Limeway Terrace road names recall this important Dorking industry.

6: Buckland Chalk Pit, 1930s *Dennis Turner Collection*

14: Brockham Limeworks, c1938

SIHG Collection

DORKING SANDPITS

A number of sandpits, which are no longer worked, may be found around Dorking, examples being at:

10 Vincent's Lane TQ 161 493 ❖
11 Shrub Hill TQ 168 495 ❖
12 Dorking Halls TQ 171 496 ❖
13 Milton Heath TQ 152 488 ❖

Also see Dorking Caves in chapter 7.

14 BROCKHAM LIMEWORKS

TQ 198 510   Kilns: **LS II** ❖

Chalk has been quarried in Brockham for many years; by the middle of the 19th century chalk quarrying and limeburning was a large industry here. The chalk was dug by hand and burnt in two batteries of kilns, east and west.

These were originally simple flare kilns but later some were converted to a design patented in 1870 by the then manager Alfred Bishop. These patent 'Brockham' kilns had a narrow pre-heating zone 'pot' above a wider calcining zone chamber. Fuel was added a little at a time via a ring of about eight vertical chutes, each with an iron lid, around the base of the pot. Lime emerged under gravity from the grate at the front of each kiln.

The western battery includes a pair of Brockham 'patent' kilns either side of the remains of a central access tunnel which probably dates from an earlier mixed-feed kiln pair. The inner ends of the coal chutes, which formed the most significant feature of the patent, may be seen.

The eastern battery appears to have been originally a number of pairs of mixed-feed flare kilns, each pair served by a central access tunnel for loading and unloading. The kilns at the north end of the range have been rebuilt as patent 'Brockham' kilns with the lower parts of the old

flare chambers modified and the access tunnels rendered redundant.

The limeworks closed in 1936 and most of the equipment and machinery was scrapped during the World War II. The features remaining were the kilns, stables, store, office and cottage. Some of these remain although some alterations were made when the buildings formed part of a narrow-gauge railway museum which subsequently moved its collection to Amberley Museum.

15 BROCKHAM HEARTHSTONE MINE

TQ 198 509   ❖

Hearthstone has been mined in the Upper Greensand south of the chalk from at least the 19th century, firstly for building stone and later for whitening hearths, floors and window sills.

The mine at Brockham had 3 drift entrances south of the limeworks and east of Bishop's Cottages. Later a brick-lined shaft was dug near to the limekilns through which stone was removed by crane; remains of this shaft are still evident. A further unlined shaft found south of the 'Pilgrim's Way' has been backfilled.

The mine was closed about 1898, reopened in 1904 and finally closed in 1925.

16 BROCKHAM BRICKWORKS

TQ 200 508   ❖

Brickmaking took place from about 1860 in the area of Gault Clay between the limeworks and the main line railway. Brockham Brickworks was established and operated at its peak at the turn of the century with a large number of brick kilns. The brickworks site also contained two hearthstone mine adits, an open quarry, remains of trackbeds and the flooded claypit. The works closed in 1910, after which the plant and equipment were sold and the structures **5** demolished. The lake in the flooded claypit is now used for angling.

17 BROCKHAM SAND PIT
TQ 202 504　　　　　　　　　　　　　■

Sand was extracted from a pit south of the present A25 road and north of the Old Reigate Road.

RAILWAYS AT BROCKHAM

There were extensive railways in the area to serve the various industries, with a siding, built in 1867, connecting to the main line between the level crossing and the cattle arch· by Pilgrim's Way Cottages.

A standard gauge track from this siding to the limekilns was used to bring in coal and take away the hearthstone and lime. This steeply-graded line was worked by a steam haulage engine built by Filmer & Mason of Guildford in 1874, housed in a building adjacent to the eastern battery of kilns. The private siding was closed in 1935.

Another standard gauge connection ran from the siding to the brickworks, and from there to the sandpit passing through the arch where the cottages now stand – neither the cottages nor the present A25 had been built at this time.

A very extensive narrow gauge network existed within the quarry areas for transporting the chalk to feed the kilns. The wagons used for this were all horse-drawn. Traces may be seen of some of the routes in the quarry.

18-19 BUILDINGS AT BROCKHAM

Bishop's Cottages (**TQ 197 509**) in Chalkpit Lane were built to house workers from the limeworks and were named after the quarry manager who invented the 'Brockham' kilns.

Stables, stores and cottage (**TQ 198 509**) still exist although the cottage was at one time used for bagging lime. A smithy was shown on earlier maps, presumably for the railway horses) and adjacent to it was a saw-pit, possibly for props for the hearthstone mine.

The limeworks site is now a public open space owned by Surrey County Council who provide a self-guided trail and interpretation boards about the industrial history as well as other aspects of the site.

20 BETCHWORTH LIMEWORKS
TQ 208 514　　　　　　　Kilns **LS II** ❖

Although chalk quarrying had been carried on here for years it was not until 1865 that large-scale lime manufacturing started with the incorporation of the Dorking Greystone Lime

Company Ltd; the peak of production taking place between 1920 and 1940. The name 'Dorking' was included in the company name to take advantage of the reputation of the lime from the earlier Dorking limeworks.

The first Hoffman kiln, which burned lime in a continuous cycle, was erected here in 1865 and operated until 1904. A second one was built in 1867 and used until 1901. In 1867 the six conical flare kilns of the southern battery were built, followed in 1872 by another six in the eastern battery. These were later converted to Bishop's patent 'Brockham' type in the 1920s and 1930s.

In 1887 two of the original flare kilns were replaced by a pair of Dietzsch kilns which had been modified from the design for cement making; ten years later a second pair were similarly converted.

When a demand for white lime for gas purification arose at the turn of the century, a new face was opened above, and to the west of, the main pit. An overhead cableway was installed to operate via pylons to the gantry between the Dietzsch kilns in the south battery. This was in use from 1901 until 1910 operated first by a 4hp Priestman paraffin engine and later by a 7hp petrol engine of the same make.

The Dietzsch kilns were last used in 1934, after which production took place in the eastern battery of kilns, most of which was upgraded during the 1950s and 1960s.

The tall brick-built Smidth kiln, built adjacent to the No 2 Hoffman kiln at the beginning of the 20th century has never been fired. It was an experimental modification to the Dietzsch kiln; it is thought that this was never used due to the sudden cessation in the demand for white lime for gasworks when it was superseded by iron oxide.

The main pit is now being used as a landfill site and it will be graded and restored for grazing.

21 BETCHWORTH HEARTHSTONE MINES
TQ 209 513　　　　　　　　　　　　■

These mines, to the east of the limeworks kiln area, operated from the 1870s until 1950. A 1ft 7in gauge railway line connected the mines to the standard gauge siding. The wagons were hauled up the steep slope out of the mine using a stationary engine. The building in which hearthstone was ground survives at the south of the site, behind the station.

RAILWAYS AT BETCHWORTH

The South Eastern Railway came to Betchworth in 1847; when the Dorking Greystone Lime Company was formed twenty years later, a siding was laid into the limeworks.

Initially the system was horse-operated but from 1871 locomotives were used and the third standard gauge locomotive on the site worked there until 1960. An extensive narrow gauge system of both 3ft 2in and 2ft 0in gauge was used to transport chalk to the kilns. There were three locomotives of the former gauge and one of the latter, all of which are now at Amberley Museum.

22 WORKERS' HOUSING AND BUILDINGS
TQ 210 517   ❖

Workers' houses in 'The Quarry' as well as some of the works buildings, including stables, still stand on the site. North-west of the limeworks in The Coombe are cottages built for the staff – New Cottages, Coombe Cottages and Western Cottages.

23 BUCKLAND TILEWORKS
TQ 237 512   ■

These were situated north of the railway off Cliftons Lane and were served by the siding which was also connected to the sandpits.

The sidings and works were extended during World War II when they were used as a munition store. Later the remaining buildings were used for storing theatrical scenery and now they are used for agricultural purposes.

24-26 BUCKLAND SANDPITS
TQ 233 510, TQ 224 506   ■

Here the Folkestone Beds of the Lower Greensand spread over a wide area and the grain size and chemical composition of the sand make it particularly suitable for glass manufacture.

The operation at Buckland, which used to be one of the largest employers in the village, was started in 1925 by the grandfather of the present owner; however since 1978 the operation has been leased to ARC Southern.

At one time the company produced up to 60 different products, a very important one being foundry sand – in fact, the propellers for the QE2 were cast in Buckland sand.

At present sand is extracted from Tapwood Pit and Park Pit to the north and south respectively of the A25. Sand from Tapwood Pit is slurried with water and pumped under the road to the processing plant in Park Pit, where the final glass sand for bottle making is produced. Construction sand is dug from Park Pit.

An earlier extraction operation took place at Colley Pit (TQ 229 512) which is now restored as a lake and used for trout fishing. Once the operations at the other pits are completed these will also be restored as lakes.

The brick and tile works received sand from the Buckland Sand and Silica Company via a 2ft 0in gauge line which ran under the railway through a narrow arch which still exists.

27 MILTON COURT CHALKPIT AND LIMEKILN
TQ 146 500   ❖

This pit was reached from the bridleway from Milton Court via Milton level crossing. Remains of a brick-built limekiln still exist within the disused chalk pit.

28 COOMBE CHALKPIT AND LIMEKILN
TQ 131 497   ❖

Remains of a limekiln may be seen in the disused pit by the North Downs Way. Lime would have been transported from the site over the level crossing on Holehill Lane leading to Westcott.

29 HACKHURST LANE CHALKPIT AND LIMEKILN
TQ 100 486   ❖

The remains of a limekiln constructed of brick and stone are to be found near where two tracks meet halfway up the Downs. The pit from which the chalk was quarried is nearby, by the path to New Barn Farm.

30 WESTCOTT SAND PIT
TQ 135 483   ❖

This disused pit is near to Rookery Drive; bands of ironstone can be clearly seen in the rock face.

31 MID-SURREY LIMEWORKS, ABINGER
TQ 114 484   ■

A proposal to open a limeworks here was drawn up in 1925 or 1926 and the works operated from the beginning of 1928. As well as greystone lump lime, white lump lime, ground lime and fine white Surrey sand were offered for sale. Water was obtained from the disused brickworks on the other side of White Down Lane.

A standard gauge siding (Evelyn's Siding) was provided to the Redhill – Guildford railway. The **7**

Bricks from Mole Valley   *Drawing: Peter Watkins*

works comprised two brick-built kilns and ancillary buildings. In May 1928 the works was put up for sale 'as a going concern' but it was not sold until June 1932, closing soon after.

Chalk was obtained from the quarry at the bottom of the Downs at **TQ 114 486** and carried to the limeworks on 2ft 0in gauge railway trucks hauled by a wire cable.

The concrete base of the kilns, which were of a French design, remains together with remnants of the siding.

32 ABINGER BRICKWORKS
TQ 110 483   ■

A brickworks which made bricks, tiles and land drains was situated north of the railway, west of White Down Lane on a narrow area of clay between the chalk and greensand. The yard closed in 1913 but the flooded claypits remain together with other minor features.

An older brickfield at **TQ 115 470** has not been used for over 150 years but Brickyard Cottages remain nearby.

33 WHITE DOWN LIMEKILN
TQ 112 480   ❖

A small brick-built limekiln may be found in the eastern verge of the lane about 200 yards south of the railway.

34 NORTH HOLMWOOD BRICKWORKS
TQ 173 474

A brick works was established here around 1870 with the original kiln being built near to the *Royal Oak* public house.

The Dorking Brick Company Ltd was registered in 1914 but no great developments occurred

until 1920-21 when F Howard Paget bought a controlling interest in the company and developed it for the production of multi-coloured, sand-faced, wire-cut bricks. Mr Paget was also part-owner of the original Crown Derby works.

The firm combined with the Sussex Brick Co in 1935 and became the Sussex and Dorking United Brick Co Ltd in 1940; this company was acquired by the Redland Group in 1958.

During World War II the works partly closed but the part which remained open produced common bricks for building air raid shelters, factories and other emergency projects.

The output from this site in the early 1960s was 15 million per year but the works closed down in 1981.

A flooded claypit remains as an ornamental feature in the Holmwood Park housing estate. The main claypit was south of Inholms Lane and the clay was transported from there to the works through an arch below the road. This arch may still be seen leading from Holmbury Drive to the claypit area which has been landscaped and planted.

The works contained a fairly extensive 2ft 0in gauge railway system operated by stationary engines and also by an automatic driverless locomotive which is now at Amberley Museum.

In 1931 the manager's Victorian house at the corner of Holmesdale Road and Spook Hill was refaced and extended using bricks from the works. This still exists as 'Brickworks House'.

35 NORTH HOLMWOOD POTTERY
TQ 168 472

Opposite North Holmwood church there was a pottery making flower pots and other coarse ware. The pond near the church was probably made by clay digging for the pottery. A row of houses in Spook Hill was until recently known as Potkiln Cottages.

36 LIMEKILN, LOGMORE LANE
TQ 154 462   ❖

The remains of a limekiln are in the verge on the west of Logmore Lane just before its junction with Coldharbour Lane.

37 BROCKHAM BRICKFIELD
TQ 202 499

J Franks had a brickfield in Kiln Lane until 1926. The site is now occupied by housing in Nutwood Avenue.

38 HENFOLD LANE LIMEKILN
TQ 183 451 ❖

Remains of a limekiln may be found in the woods opposite 'Kiln House', south of Four-wents Road.

39 LEIGH LIMEKILN
TQ 238 468 ❖

This limekiln at Butler's Shaw is south of the concrete track from Bury's Court where the woodland ends. The brick-built kiln may be seen next to a pollarded oak tree which is thought to be over 500 years old.

40 HOLMBURY ST MARY BRICKWORKS
TQ 111 446

A brickworks was established here in 1826 which produced pink Felday bricks for 62 years. For the first 40 years the bricks were exported from the village (Christ Church, Woking was built of Holmbury bricks) but with the development of Holmbury St Mary they began to be used for the large houses being built in the new village.

The brickworks was on the edge of Feldemore woods behind the houses in the main road. In 1888 it was bought by Edwin Waterhouse (founder of Price, Waterhouse) who closed it down when he built Feldemore House, now Belmont School.

41-44 SANDSTONE QUARRIES, LEITH HILL
TQ 147 442 ❖
TQ 146 438 ❖
TQ 132 433 ❖

A number of quarries from which sandstone for building was extracted existed around the Leith Hill area; these were mainly used during the 19th century.

Holbury St Mary church was built in 1879 using local stone with Bath stone dressings whilst Holmwood church, built from 1838, used stone from Coldharbour and Leith Hill.

Stone is still quarried occasionally from High Ashes quarry at TQ 128 437.

45 BRICKWORKS AT BEARE GREEN
TQ 176 437

In the latter part of the 19th century a brickworks operated south of the Old Horsham Road between Holmwood station and the White Hart. Bricks were still made in the area until 1938. A pond remains on the site.

46 BEARE GREEN BRICKWORKS
TQ 184 424 *See photo on page 12* ∎

This was opened in the 1930s and became part

39: Limekiln at Leigh   *Photo: Chris Shepheard*

of the Redland Group in 1958 when they took over the Sussex and Dorking Brick Company. Until that date the works employed about 40 brickmakers producing only hand-made bricks.

Around 1963 they invested in a Hubert machine which produced simulated hand-made bricks enabling them to reduce the number of hand makers to 10. At that time the works was producing 120,000 'Weald-Made' bricks per week of which only 20,000 were truly hand-made.

The 'brick knot' outside Redland's offices in Reigate is made with Beare Green bricks.

In mid-1993 the works closed and the production and staff moved to the Wealden works at Horsham for machine-made bricks whilst the hand-making operation transferred to Swanage. Following closure the kiln has been demolished but other buildings remain.

47 SOUTH HOLMWOOD BRICKWORKS
TQ 184 424 ∎

This is on the same site as the Beare Green works and uses the same claypit. It was built in 1974 to replace the North Holmwood works and it made Dorking multi-coloured stock bricks using an extrusion plant capable of producing 520,000 bricks per week.

In 1985 a second gas-fired kiln and additional dryers were installed bringing the production capacity to one million bricks per week.

48 NEWDIGATE BRICKWORKS
TQ 203 424 ∎

Although individual brick and tile makers had operated in Newdigate for many years, **9** large-scale brickmaking started in 1928. The works in Hogspudding Lane was started by Frederick Corroyer, who lived at 'Hatchetts', as a means of providing employment for local men at a time of high unemployment.

They produced very hard, steely-blue, hand-made bricks until their closure in 1974. The bricks from Newdigate had an **N** in the frog whereas those from Beare Green had **BG**.

The brickworks closed during World War II after which Frederick Corroyer sold it to Barence Facings. It was later bought by Woodside Brickworks of Croydon, then Hall & Co and finally by Ready Mixed Concrete. In 1980 RMC applied to use the site for landfill purposes but this was refused because of the poor approach road.

Some of the brickworks buildings remain in 1995 together with a large lake formed from the flooded claypit. There are proposals for further clay-digging and brickmaking to take place on the site after a lapse of over 20 years.

49 NEW PLACE BRICKYARD
TQ 113 419   ■

This brickfield was operated by Messrs. W and G King in conjunction with the White Down Brickyard at Abinger. The tenancies of both yards expired in 1913 when both were put up for sale together with large stocks of bricks and tiles as well as brickmaking machinery.

The site remains in Cotton Row, south of Holmbury Farm, the house on the site being called 'Old Kiln House'.

50 BRICK AND TILE WORKS, CAPEL
TQ 165 405

Lee Steeres of Jayes Park had a brick and tile works east of Ockley station from which up to 3 wagons of bricks a week were dispatched by rail. The works closed in 1914.

Other works in the area were at Old Kiln Farm (TQ 169 403), near Henhurst Cross Lane (TQ 164 421) and in Weare Street (TQ 162 388).

51 AUCLAYE BRICKWORKS
TQ 168 389

This works at Knoll Farm, Capel operated between 1930 and 1964, using hand-dug clay to make hand-made bricks. The company advertised 'hand-made, multi-colour, clamp-burned stocks'. Bricks from this works were used on many buildings in the area; they are recognisable by the **AB** moulded into the frog.

When the Newdigate brickworks closed, Ian Benstead bought much of the plant and

52: Clock House Brickworks, Capel
Photo: Butterley Brick Ltd

equipment and reopened the Auclaye works in 1974/5 and operated for about eight years using machine-dug clay. The buildings and plant were sold in 1983 and, although they remain, no brickmaking has taken place since then.

An earlier brickworks using the same name used to operate on the east of the A24 at TQ 172 401.

52 CLOCKHOUSE BRICKWORKS
TQ 175 386   ■

This was built in 1930 by the Clockhouse Brick Company to make high-class hollow clay blocks from the local Weald clay. The name of the works was derived from the clock on the old estate house which operated a bell to summon the staff to work. The works comprised an extrusion plant and a coal-fired zig-zag kiln, so called because the fire, instead of traversing around the kiln as in the Hoffman type, zig-zagged across from chamber to chamber.

The London Brick Company took over the business in 1942 and in 1948 they built a second zig-zag kiln and dryers, followed in 1952 by an oil-fired tunnel kiln, by which time this was the largest works in the world engaged solely in the manufacture of solid clay blocks.

In 1966 the zig-zag kilns closed and by 1970 the number of employees had fallen from 250 to 60 and these kilns had been demolished.

In 1977 a new tunnel kiln and clay preparation machinery by Morando Impiati of Italy were installed to make 'simulated hand-made' bricks. The following year a Dutch-made Hubert machine was installed to make stock bricks named 'Ruspers'; by 1982 production of three types of brick averaged 300,000 bricks per week.

In 1984 the London Brick Company was acquired by the Hanson Trust and subsequently the non-Fletton brickmaking interests, including Clockhouse Works, were transferred to Butterley Brick. Butterley installed further equipment to increase the output to one million bricks per week together with up to 10,000 special shaped bricks.

The bricks for the Mole Valley District Council offices at Pippbrook, Dorking, were made at Clockhouse brickworks.

53 SMOKEJACKS BRICKWORKS, WALLISWOOD
TQ 116 372   ■

This started in the 1920s as a small clamp yard producing about 25,000 bricks per week after the site had been bought from the Wotton estates for its timber.

In 1933 it was abandoned by the Brockham Brick Company who had moved from Brockham via Beare Green to Smokejacks.

The Ockley Brick, Tile and Pottery Company was set up who proceeded to install continuous Hoffman type kilns which were converted in 1939 to oil firing.

During the war brickmaking ceased and the works was used as a government food store.

With the modern automated plant an output of about one million bricks per week would now be possible although tiles and hand-made bricks are also produced here. The kilns are now fired by natural gas.

In 1988 what had become the Ockley Brick Company was acquired by Blue Circle and is now part of Ockley Building Products Ltd. who also produce bricks near Sittingbourne in Kent.

In the 1940s a number of dinosaur bones were found in the claypit, the first such bones from Surrey to go to the British Museum.

Bricks from this works can be recognised by the double diamond pattern in the frog.

54 HOOKWOOD BRICKWORKS
TQ 271 426

A brickworks was operating in Reigate Road in the early part of the 20th century on the site now occupied by the Tesco Superstore; there was another brickfield in the area operating at about the same time at TQ 256 433.

BRICKWORKS IN CHARLWOOD
There were a number of small works in Charlwood, for example at TQ 224 400 and TQ 239 406 until the 1930s and in Ifield Road at TQ 238 400 until 1958.

55 CHARLWOOD STONE
TQ 23 41

Charlwood Stone, or Paludina Limestone, used to be dug from bell pits in the area of Stan Hill and Norwood Hill, where ponds remain.

Charlwood stone was used for building St Nicholas' church (**LS I**), the cage (**LS II**) and the village hall but most noticeable are the stone paths or causeways (**LSII**) radiating from the church.

A large slab of the stone about 9ft by 3ft and 8in deep exists in the garden of Dormer Cottage. This is cut as a trough with a drainhole; its purpose is uncertain.

WEALDEN IRON
Iron was produced in the Wealden area of Surrey, Sussex and Kent from pre-historic and Roman times but the industry began to decline in the early part of the 16th century. As coal replaced charcoal in the smelting process, the iron industry moved from the Weald to coal-mining areas further north.

Of the water-powered sites which have been identified, the following are in Mole Valley.

56 ABINGER HAMMER FORGE
TQ 097 474   ❖

In 1550 Edward and Thomas Elrington bought the manor of Abinger with its extensive woodlands and by 1557 they had built an iron mill on the site of a corn mill.

This was the most northerly of the Wealden iron works, producing at its peak 150 tons of

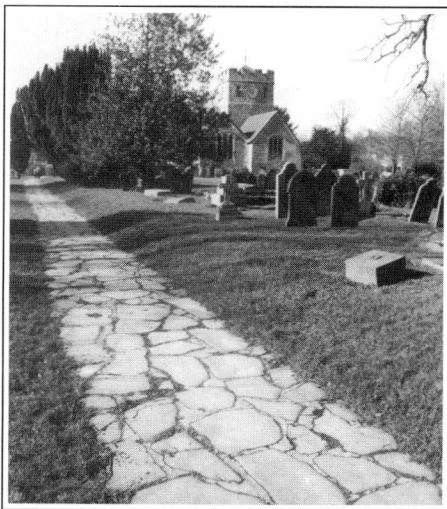

55: Charlwood Stone path, Charlwood

56: Forge Hole, Abinger Hammer

Photo: Chris Shepheard

wrought iron per year. The forge ceased to operate in 1787. The remains of the pond bay with the masonry of the old forge hole may be seen in the bank between the Kingfisher farm shop and Martin Grant's offices. The site of the hammer pond was redeveloped as watercress beds.

Some slag from Abinger Hammer is displayed in Guildford Museum.

57 EWOOD FURNACE AND FORGE
TQ 200 446 ❖

The ironworks here had been built by 1553 when the manor of Ewood was sold to George and Christopher Darrell, who leased it a year later to John Stapley and George Newman. Darrell, however, maintained an interest, for in 1557 he employed staff and in 1563 he was licensed to cut wood regardless of statute regulations.

The long pond bay, which is a County Site of Archaeological Importance, remains with masonry culverts together with the dry pond of up to 90 acres.

The iron works closed early in the 17th century and a corn mill operated on the site, but this had stopped working by the next century.

58 LEIGH HAMMER FORGE
TQ 222 461 ❖

The lease on this site was transferred to George and Christopher Darrell in 1554 by which time the ironworks was already in operation. Subsequently the forge was operated in conjunction with the works at Ewood.

Cinder and charcoal have been found in the area of Leigh Bridge but no other features remain. A slab of cast-iron 12" by 9" by 2" was found in 1930 and given to the Geological Museum; around the same time one of the cams which lifted the hammer was found and is now on display in Guildford Museum.

46: Loading a kiln at Beare Green Brickworks

Photo: Redland plc

WINDMILLS

No working windmill remains in Mole Valley. The only mill which is at all complete and able to operate is Lowfield Heath mill which was dismantled from its original site (now in Sussex) and re-erected in the grounds of Gatwick Zoo and Aviaries.

Although traces of some windmills have disappeared completely, the remains of a number still exist.

59: Shiremark Mill, Capel, 1930s
Photo: Dennis Turner Collection

59 SHIREMARK MILL, CAPEL
TQ 172 376 ■

This mill was exactly on the Surrey-Sussex border and about 100 yards west of the Dorking–Worthing road.

The smock mill was built in 1774 using materials from the demolished mill at Clark's Green (**TQ 176 398**). In 1777 David Southow offered for sale his 'newly-built' windmill with 'all her gears and other utensils fit for business'.

By 1800 the mill had had five owners and in 1802 it was bought by the Stone family who regularly worked it until 1914. It was finally abandoned after World War I.

In 1950 the Capel Parish Council approached the owner and the Society for the Protection of Ancient Buildings in an endeavour to save the mill whose condition had deteriorated. Detailed drawings were produced and a model was made, but by 1956 the sails had fallen down and no restoration took place.

During the winter of 1972 the mill was burnt down and all that remains of what was, with the exception of Outwood, the last Surrey smock mill is the octagonal brick base.

60 CHARLWOOD WINDMILL
TQ 245 409 ■

This was a tall white weather-boarded smock mill replacing an earlier mill blown down in 1703. The later mill was burnt in 1901 leaving the octagonal brick base.

Before the fire a portable steam engine had been employed to drive one of the four pairs of stones when there was insufficient wind to operate the mill. After the fire a Hornsby steam engine was installed which operated one pair of stones in the roofed-over brick base until 1920. Although the miller's cottage and other buildings were demolished, the base was converted into a house around 1934 for the chauffeur of the

61: Lowfield Heath Windmill, Charlwood
Photo: Chris Shepheard **13**

owner of the property. 'Mill Cottage' still stands as a private dwelling.

61 LOWFIELD HEATH WINDMILL
TQ 235 407 **LS II**

The development of Gatwick Airport resulted in the virtual disappearance of the village of Lowfield Heath except for the church and windmill. An opportunity came for residents of Charlwood to restore the mill which had become derelict, but in order to allow public access to the restored structure it meant dismantling the mill and erecting it elsewhere.

The 'Friends of Lowfield Heath Windmill' raised the money and carried out the restoration of the mill which has been re-erected at Russ Hill in the car park of Gatwick Zoo and Aviaries. The dismantling started in 1987. Re-erection commenced in 1988 and the restored mill was officially opened in 1990.

The white post mill with tailpole, dating from about 1762, worked until 1880 and was renovated in 1936. At its Lowfield Heath site (**TQ 271 398**) it was in Surrey until the boundary changes of 1974 and now that it has been re-erected in Charlwood it is once more in its original county.

The restoration is not finally complete in 1994 but the mill is open to visitors on summer Sunday afternoons.

62 HOLMWOOD MILL
TQ 175 452

Here there was a post mill which had one pair of patent sails. It had a brick-built roundhouse 27 feet in diameter. The 17th century mill broke down in 1870 and was demolished in 1873. 'Mill House' was built on the site of the mill. The alter rails in South Holmwood church were made from oak from the demolished mill.

63 SHELLWOOD MILL
TQ 211 454

An early Shellwood Mill was burnt down and a new post mill built in 1795. Although another fire destroyed the house and outbuildings in 1826, the mill remained and continued to operate until 1907. It was demolished about 10 years later except for the roundhouse which was used as a pig sty until it too was demolished about 1936.

The house called 'Shellwood Mill' is on the opposite side of the road to the mill site.

64 OCKLEY MILL
TQ 147 395

This mill stood on Elmer's Hill, close to Elmer's Farm with its pond, adjacent to the A29 at the south end of Ockley village.

The smock mill was built in 1803 and ceased working in 1912. From that time it deteriorated until it finally collapsed in 1944.

The octagonal brick base remains, covered by a corrugated iron roof, and is used as a farm store.

64: Elmer's Mill, Ockley
Left: remains in 1995   *Photo Chris Shepheard*
Above: The Mill, C1900   *Photo: Goodness Gracious*

WATERMILLS

Many water-driven mills existed in the area. Because of this the number of windmills was comparatively few.

The two main rivers in the District are the Mole, flowing south to north from the Gatwick area in Sussex to the Thames at Molesey, and the Tillingbourne flowing east to west from the slopes of Leith Hill above Wotton to join the Wey at Shalford.

The mills on the Mole and its tributaries will be described first, then those on the Tillingbourne, followed by mills on streams flowing southwards to feed the river Arun.

RIVER MOLE
65 FLANCHFORD MILL
TQ 235 479   ■

This mill is on Wallace Brook just before it joins the Mole and is, therefore, a few yards outside Mole Valley District. It is an ivy-covered wood and brick building, and although now derelict, some of the machinery and the ruined waterwheel are still there.

A mill has been on this site since the 13th century, the present mill being built in the middle of the 18th century. It operated until World War II with two pairs of stones.

There are two 1930s cottages attached to the mill; the mill pond is used for breeding fish.

66 WONHAM MILL
TQ 224 496   Mill House **LS II**   ■

Another mill just on the District boundary, this has mill ponds fed from the Shag Brook and discharges into the Mole 100 yards away.

The tenants from 1845 until 1930 were the Bowyer family. In the 1890s Ernest Bowyer, whilst retaining the overshot wheel, installed a Simon roller mill powered by a 16hp Hornsby oil engine. In 1914 the structure was enlarged by the addition of a four-storey extension to the main mill, and the old stable block was replaced by a brick building.

Milling ceased in 1930 and the Millers' Mutual Association took over the business, selling the mill machinery in 1937. The buildings were

66: Wonham Mill   *Photo: Chris Shepheard*

requisitioned for grain storage during World War II and since 1946 they have been used by William Lillico & Son Ltd for storage of animal feedstuff and grain drying.

The complex remains as a very interesting collection of building types and ages next to the mill pond.

67 EWOOD MILL
TQ 200 447

This mill on a tributary of the Mole was on the site of a Wealden ironworks. A corn-mill operated here after the decline of the ironworks but it was probably demolished in the early part of the 18th century.

The very large mill pond was drained in 1840 but traces of the dam may be seen near 'Ewood Mill Cottage' with the level area of the mill pond behind.

68 CASTLE MILL
TQ 179 501   **LS II**   ■

This is on the site of a Doomsday mill; in 1649 it formed part of the manor of West Betchworth and in 1760 it belonged to Betchworth Castle estate.

The corn-mill was enlarged in 1836 with a two-storey weather-boarded extension; at the beginning of the 20th century it had four pairs of stones. After a fire in 1933 the amount of milling was reduced and by 1949 the last remaining operative pair of stones, which had been producing animal feed, stopped. The mill closed in 1952.

The waterwheel and machinery which are there today were installed in 1829. The cast-iron wheel is 16' 10" in diameter and 6' 2" wide. The iron pit wheel, 10' 6" in diameter, was cast in two halves and has wooden teeth. The vertical shaft is probably older than the iron machinery and appears to have been cut from a pine tree.

The mill was restored for residential use by architect Michael Manser after he bought it in a derelict state in 1969. In 1974 he earned a European Heritage Award and a year later the

68: Castle Mill, Dorking, in 1830

Surrey Archaeological Society

Civic Trust's Architectural Heritage Year Award for the project.

In 1978 the owner attempted to operate the wheel. However, as the river level had been lowered by 5 feet the mill race had to be lowered to correspond. The breast-shot wheel became undershot.

THE PIPPBROOK

The Pippbrook rises near the Tillingbourne in Holmwood but having flowed northwards towards Westcott it turns eastwards, joining the Mole below Box Hill near Pixham Lane. A number of watermills operated on this comparatively small stream.

69-70 ROOKERY MILLS

TQ 132 481   ■
TQ 132 479

There were two flour mills in the Rookery estate before 1729, one on the embankment between the two lakes and one below the lower lake.

There is no trace of the upper mill but the mill building of the lower mill has been converted to a private house.

71 WESTCOTT MILL

TQ 137 486   'The Old Mill House' **LS II** ■

This mill needed a large mill pond which was constructed in the 17th century with having an area of six acres. The present mill building was erected in 1850; the mill operated until 1909, and the machinery was sold in 1912. The building was then used as a fishing lodge by Mr Brooke (of the tea company) for fishing in the mill pond.

The mill is now converted to a private house (**LS II**) but the water still flows through the wheel pit and the large mill pond remains.

72 MILTON COURT MILL

TQ 150 492

This mill, by the entrance to Milton Court, was demolished after World War II. However, the mill cottage remains just inside the entrance to the grounds with the mill pond on the opposite side of the farm track.

73 PARSONAGE MILL

TQ 161 496

When this mill was demolished in 1959 it was one of the oldest in the county although it had ceased to be water-driven around the time of World War I.

A roller mill on the site is used for animal feedstuff but there are now light industrial units on the site of the watermill.

74 PIPPBROOK MILL
TQ 169 499   **LS II** ■

This building was constructed in 1979. The original mill caught fire and was gutted, but being a listed building it was rebuilt exactly as before.

The mill actually stopped working in 1932 and its mill pond is now part of Meadowbank recreation ground.

75 PIXHAM MILL
TQ 173 506   **LS II** ■

The present three-storey brick building dates from 1837 replacing an earlier mill. The machinery was driven by a 13ft diameter overshot wheel which was 10ft wide. The mill was operated by the Attlee family (who also ran Parsonage Mill) from 1882 until milling ceased in 1910, the machinery being removed in 1937 for use in a Sussex mill.

During World War II Moss Bros, the tailors, used the building as a warehouse but it is now converted to a private house, but the water channels remain.

Pixham Mill Cottage (**LS II**) was built in the first half of the 17th century.

RIVER MOLE
LEATHERHEAD TOWN MILL
TQ 164 563

Returning to the river Mole, the next mill was just upstream of Leatherhead Town Bridge. Details of this mill will be found in the chapter on 'Other Industries', site 235.

76 FETCHAM MILL
TQ 160 563

Until it was burnt down in 1917 this was the principal corn-mill for the area. The 12ft diameter internally-mounted overshot water-wheel drove three pairs of stones as well as a pump to supply water to Fetcham Park.

The mill was driven by the overflow from a pond, formed by several strong springs, which flows into the Mole a few yards from the mill.

Mizen Brothers, the well-known Surrey market gardeners, had land near the mill pond in the 1920s when there were 8 acres of watercress beds in the spring-fed ponds and 15 acres of glasshouses for growing salad crops. This ceased in 1957 when the land was taken over by the East Surrey Water Company and the Leatherhead bus garage.

77 SLYFIELD MILL
TQ 133 579

This was the site of a Doomsday Mill, and by 1614 there were two corn mills and a fulling mill on the Slyfield estate.

235: Leatherhead Town Mill   See entry on page 55

The last mill to be erected here was a three-storey brick and timber building dating from the second half of the 18th century. It ceased operating in 1846 after which it was demolished. Traces of the watercourses may still be seen.

During landscaping works on the estate in 1969 some buried timbers were found which formed the outer rim of a waterwheel 14 feet in diameter, together with the axle shaft. These are assumed to be the remains of an earlier waterwheel.

Details of six further mills on the river Mole are given in *A Guide to the Industrial Archaeology of the Borough of Elmbridge* by Rowland Baker, published by SIHG.

THE TILLINGBOURNE

The Tillingbourne at one time had about 30 watermills along its eleven miles. These were used for, among other industries, milling corn, wiremaking, fulling cloth and making gunpowder.

The sources of the Tillingbourne are on the north slopes of Leith Hill, the two main ones being the springs at the head of Broadmoor valley and those near Abinger Bottom. The two streams flow northwards with series of weirs and ponds before turning westwards and combining near Wotton House.

78 BROOKMILL
TQ 139 455   ❖

This was the site of a 16th century mill which was the nucleus of the hamlet of Broadmoor. From this area a leat was constructed in c1738 to feed the ornamental cascade at TQ 138 458 together with ornamental fountains and other features.

79 POND BAY
TQ 127 451   ❖

The remains of a pond bay may be seen here fed by the Abinger Bottom springs. It is possible that this was the site of a gunpowder mill.

80 FRIDAY STREET
TQ 128 458   ❖

The large picturesque mill pond served a corn-mill from the late 16th century, and possibly an earlier gunpowder mill, until 1736 when Sir John Evelyn closed the mill and moved the owner to Abinger Mill. The mill house, Pond Cottage (**LS II**), remains below the dam.

From the pond at Friday Street this branch of the Tillingbourne flows down through Wotton

House grounds in a series of landscaped artificial fish ponds; the construction of these was the reason for the closure of Friday Street mill.

At TQ 125 465 a leat leaves the main stream to feed the fountains in the garden of Wotton House.

81 WOTTON
TQ 122 470   ■

Near Wotton House traces have been found of 17th century wire mills and gunpowder mills. During the early part of the 17th century the works comprised a copper mill for converting copper ingots into brass, and a wire works for turning the brass into goods such as chains, fish hooks and curtain rings.

82 ABINGER MILL
TQ 110 471   ■

Abinger Mill (also known as Crane's Mill and Elwix Mill) dates from the 16th century and was used for many purposes during its lifetime. From 1589 until at least 1622 it was used for gunpowder production, then for making copper utensils until 1667 when the site reverted to flour milling.

Milling stopped around 1885 and the mill was demolished at the time of World War I but the attractive mill house (**LS II**) survives with the remains of a wheel pit in the garden.

83 PADDINGTON MILL
TQ 100 472   ■

This Victorian brick-built corn mill operated until 1915 when it contined two pairs of stones. The last operators were R & J Coe, the local watercress growers, whose watercress beds were west of the mill.

The 10ft diameter overshot wheel was dismantled many years ago; the 9in diameter shaft remains together with the iron pentrough dated 1867 but the semi-derelict brick, weatherboarded and tiled mill building is empty.

In the 14th century there was a fulling mill on this site.

84 ABINGER FORGE MILL
TQ 097 474

The forge was active during the period of iron-working in the area and when this ceased in 1788 attempts were made to use the mill for gunpowder, papermaking and corn milling but none succeeded.

The mill site has been developed but the masonry of the old forge hole may be seen.

Details of other mills on the Tillingbourne downstream to the river Wey at Shalford will be found in *A Guide to the Industrial History of Guildford and its Borough* by Francis Haveron also published by SIHG.

THE NORTH RIVER

The other mills in Mole Valley District are on the North River which flows into the River Arun.

85 FOREST GREEN MILL
TQ 119 416 ■

Situated at the end of Mill Lane, Forest Green, this is a three-storeyedbrick building with a slate roof. A mill has existed here since the 18th century and the present one operated until 1915. It had an overshot wheel but this and the internal machinery have disappeared. The wheel pit is still evident under a large concrete slab. The large mill pond area can be seen but it now flows directly into the stream rather than through the wheel pit. The weir remains in the stream.

In the early 1920s the mill was bought for residential purposes and most of the machinery was removed. Since the 1930s the mill has been used as an educational field centre and from 1983 by William Ellis School which has recently extended the buildings and created a nature reserve and lake in part of the old mill pond area.

86 OAKWOOD MILL
TQ 136 383 ❖

This was by Oakwood Mill Farm, south of Ockley on the west side of Stane Street.

The building was of a similar age to Forest Green Mill but of wooden construction. It operated until 1922 having a 17' 0" diameter, 5' 6" wide waterwheel with a large mill pond formed north of the mill.

Much of the mill was dismantled in 1947 in order to use the materials to repair other farm buildings and all traces were lost after the gales of 1987 and 1990. The site of the mill building is under the rebuilt farm track but the site of the pond and millstream may be discerned.

87 VANN LAKE
TQ 156 393 ❖

This large expanse of water by Vann House was made by damming a stream which flows into the North River. The original purpose was to provide power for a linen mill in the 18th century, but the mill was never built. Nor does the proposal to generate electricity for Vann House appear to have been carried out.

The lake is now a nature reserve run by the Surrey Wildlife Trust.

right: 273: Street Furniture, Dorking. See page 61
Photo: Chris Shepheard

far right: 92: Signpost on Old Reigate Road, Dorking See page 21
Drawing: Peter Watkins

ROADS AND BRIDGES

The Roman road, Stane Street, linked London and Chichester and would have run south of Ashtead, crossed Mickleham Downs, and then the River Mole at Burford before going through Dorking and Holmwood to take the route of the present A29 through Ockley almost to the present county boundary.

In later years the main route south from Dorking would have been through Coldharbour to Ockley by very narrow, and often impassable, lanes. In the early 18th century Horsham residents asserted that the quickest route to London was via Canterbury. However, in 1755 the turnpike road was built from Epsom to Horsham via Dorking. From Leatherhead it followed the Mole valley to Mickleham, where it crossed the river at Burford Bridge, just past the *Fox and Hounds* Inn (now the *Burford Bridge Hotel*), then ran across the Pippbrook, along London Road, High Street and South Street to Horsham Road. The road then crossed the Bentsbrook and went through North, Mid and South Holmwood to Capel.

The early east-west route through Leatherhead followed the track known as the Harroway which forded the Mole near the present bridge although a bridge has probably existed here since the 13th century. The Leatherhead to Guildford turnpike was opened in 1758 and that from Leatherhead to Kingston in 1811.

The west-east route through Dorking followed the present A25 to the town but crossed the Mole by Boxhill Bridge and then turned right along the Old Reigate Road which continued to the right of what is now Arkle Manor public house passing through Betchworth to join the present road at Buckland.

88 LEATHERHEAD BRIDGE
TQ 163 563   **LSII** ❖

In the 17th and 18th centuries there were so many complaints about the state of the existing bridge that in 1760 it was kept locked and keys were only issued to those who paid for them. Others had to use the ford.

In 1774 the Surrey justices recommended that Leatherhead Bridge should be repaired and enlarged. When the bridge came under the control of the county authorities in 1782, it was rebuilt by the County Surveyor of Surrey, George Gwilt. He reconstructed and widened the bridge using the existing medieval stone piers and old bricks from Ashtead Park.

Gwilt, with the contractor George Fentiman, rebuilt the medieval bridges at Godalming, Cobham and Leatherhead, all to a similar design using red brickwork with Portland stone cappings and string courses. Leatherhead Bridge is the longest of the three, with an overall length of 312ft. It has 14 equal segmental three-ring brick arches of 13ft 4in span and corbelled pedestrian refuges.

The Surrey County Council refurbished the bridge in 1989 but its appearance is substantially

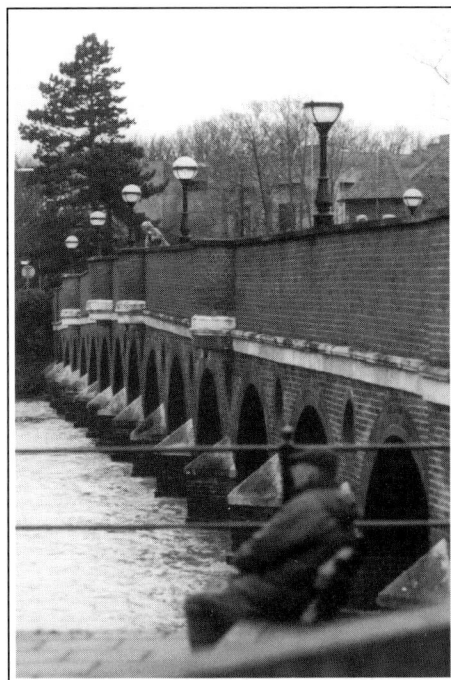

88: Leatherhead Bridge   *Photo: Chris Shepheard*

91: Young Street   Photo: Chris Shepheard

unchanged. The ford remained until the western approach was destroyed when the electricity works was constructed and the eastern approach remained until Minchin Close was built after World War II.

89 MICKLEHAM BY- PASS
TQ 167 550 to TQ 170 501 ❖

This road was commenced in 1935 and embodied many of the latest ideas in road construction, including dual carriageways, cycle tracks and accommodation for pedestrians. Ironically in the 1990s the northern part of the south-bound carriageway has been reduced to one lane as a speed restricting measure following a number of accidents on the bends.

The whole section from Givons Grove round-about to Westhumble Street was completed in 1937. The section south of this into Dorking was constructed in 1964.

90 BURFORD BRIDGE
TQ 171 518 ❖

When the Leatherhead Dorking road became a turnpike in 1775 Burford Bridge was con-structed. In the middle of the next century this three-arch bridge was widened and raised to avoid flooding problems.

When the by-pass was constructed in 1935 and the present bridge was built, traces of the Roman ford on Stane Street were found.

91 YOUNG STREET
TQ 151 549 to 167 550 ❖

This road connecting the A246 with Givons Grove was built by Canadian Royal Engineers in 1941 during World War II under the command of Major Young.

The narrow roads of Leatherhead caused congestion to military traffic and so the Canadian Road Construction Company based at Oxshott Brickworks was employed to complete the by-pass. The work involved a wooden bridge over the Mole (replaced by a Bailey bridge in 1952 after flood damage) and modification to a small existing archway through the railway embankment. This narrow arch meant that lights were needed to regulate traffic through it.

Subsequently the road has been widened and realigned and a new river bridge and railway arch have been constructed.

A cairn by Givons Grove roundabout records that the road was opened in 1941 by William Mackenzie King, Prime Minister of Canada, and that the rebuilt road was opened in 1978 by Paul Martin, High Commissioner for Canada.

92 BOXHILL BRIDGE
TQ 183 503 ❖

This was a four-arch bridge with further arches under the approach road to cater for the river in flood.

The bridge was on the old Reigate Road and became redundant when the road was diverted through Betchworth Park in 1927. In 1968 the bridge was swept away in the floods and replaced by a steel footbridge. The abutments of the road bridge remain.

By the old road, at **TQ 183 504**, there is a broken road sign pointing to Reigate with **STONE AND TURNER, DORKING** and **STICK NO BILLS** cast into the column.

93 DEEPDENE BRIDGE
TQ 186 503 ❖

This bridge over the Mole was built in 1927 when the old Reigate Road and Boxhill Bridge were by passed.

94 BOROUGH BRIDGE, BROCKHAM
TQ 196 496   LS▯ ❖

This narrow brick bridge over the Mole was built in 1737 by Richard and Thomas Skilton and strengthened by Surrey County Council in 1991.

Although the narrow bridge was retained after the 1991 works, a new wooden arched footbridge was provided on the downstream side.

The road bridge has four main arches with three further arches in the south abutment and a tunnel in the north abutment for flood relief. **21**

95: Packhorse Bridge, Brockham *Photo: C Shepheard*

99: Betchworth Bridge and raised Causeway
Photo: Chris Shepheard

95 PACKHORSE BRIDGE, BROCKHAM
TQ 199 497 ❖

A small brick bridge crosses the Mole 400m upstream from Borough Bridge. Although rebuilt by Surrey County Council in 1991-2, this was an old packhorse bridge on the route to Betchworth; adjacent to it is a smaller brick arch over a mill stream although the mill has long gone.

96 SHELL BRIDGE, LEATHERHEAD
TQ 167 560 **LS II** ■

Henry Crabb Boulton, who lived at Thorncroft Manor, had the grounds designed by 'Capability' Brown who cut a canal to create Thorncroft Island. Part of the landscaping scheme involved this 'shell' bridge constructed of brick and flint with keystones and abutments decorated with clam shells. The bridge may be seen from the footpath between Thorncroft Bridge and the Town Bridge.

97 PRESSFORWARD BRIDGE
TQ 168 543 ❖

This bridge, also known as Locke's Bridge,

carries the northern drive to Norbury Park over the Mole. The four-arched bridge was built around 1780 and strengthened by Surrey County Council in 1990.

98 WEIR BRIDGE
TQ 170 537 **LS II** ❖

The southern entrance to Norbury Park was originally either by a watersplash or a dilapidated footbridge. By 1840 the footbridge was unsafe and a road bridge, today known as Weir Bridge, was built. Weir Lodge was also constructed at the entrance to the property but this was demolished when the A24 was dualled in 1937. The three-arched brick bridge has wrought iron railings and sculptured masks on the central keystones.

99 BETCHWORTH BRIDGE
TQ 211 495 ❖

This three-arched bridge which carries The Street over the Mole was built in 1842 and refurbished by Surrey County Council in 1993. The northern approach has the footway on a raised causeway in case of flooding.

100: Bridge in Ashtead Park

Photo: Chris Shepheard

100 PRIVATE ROAD BRIDGE, ASHTEAD

TQ 191 582 **LS II** ❖

This bridge carries Rookery Hill through Ashtead Park. It dates from c1880 and is constructed of Portland stone with cast, iron beams and brackets. Beneath the bridge there is a small electricity distribution substation.

101 STANE STREET

TQ 195 568 to 180 540 **AM** ❖
TQ 165 455 ❖
TQ 153 416 to 139 381 ❖

A section of Stane Street may be followed as a footpath from Thirty Acres Barn, Ashtead, to Juniper Hill, Mickleham. A section of the road through Redlands Wood, Holmwood was excavated by the Surrey Archaeological Society in 1935 and the stretch marked with iron posts. A length of 120 feet was restored to its original condition then covered with turves, but the marker posts have disappeared and it is not clear exactly where the restored section is. This stretch of the A29 through Ockley follows the route of Stane Street.

TOLL GATES

When the London to Horsham turnpike was established, toll gates were set up in Epsom Road, Leatherhead and on either side of Dorking. The Leatherhead toll house disappeared with the construction of the Knoll roundabout and the by-pass. North of Dorking the toll gate was at Giles Green opposite the *Beehive* public house; although no longer an inn *The Beehive* remains as a private house (**LS II**) at TQ 170 511. South of the town the toll gate was originally at the end of Hampstead Road but it was moved c.1857 to a position south of Harrow Road so that people living in the new development on Tower Hill would not have to pay to go into Dorking. Beyond Dorking there were toll gates north of Beare Green at TQ 174 443 on the Horsham Road and near the junction north of Hale House at TQ 139 381 on Stane Street. A toll bar was also in position at the western end of West Street.

104 TOLL GATE, BETCHWORTH PARK

TQ 184 501 ❖

The coach road through Betchworth Park was a toll road from the 19th century to c.1930. Part of the swivel gate of the pedestrian turnstile at the northern end of the road remains in position.

104: Tolgate, Betchworth Park   *Photo: C Shepheard*

MILESTONES, MILEPOSTS ETC.

105 LEATHERHEAD

TQ 165 595 ❖

In the verge on the west side of Kingston Road near Pachesham Park there is a milestone from the 1811 turnpike. It is inscribed:

ROYAL EXCHANGE 19 MILES, WHITEHALL 17¼ MILES, HYDE PARK 16 MILES, PARISH OF LEATHERHEAD, TO SURBITON 3 MILES, KINGSTON 6 MILES, TO LEATHERHEAD 2 MILES, DORKING 7 MILES.

106 GREAT BOOKHAM

TQ 134 543 ❖

In the trees south of the A246 near Brodrick Grove is a milestone from the 1758 turnpike to Guildford. There is no inscription but it appears to have had a cast-iron plate which has been removed.

107 FETCHAM

TQ 160 560 ❖

In the verge outside the *Rising Sun* public **23**

III: Milestone on Stane Street, at Ockley
Drawing: Peter Watkins

house is another milestone from the 1758 turnpike inscribed:

FETCHAM, LONDON 19, LEATHERHEAD ½, GUILDFORD 11.

108 FETCHAM
TQ 149 549 ■

A milestone used to be situated on the south side of the A246 near the top of Hawks Hill. What appears to be this milestone is to be found in the front garden of a house in Swallow Lane, Holmwood; it is inscribed

FETCHAM, LONDON 20, LEATHERHEAD 1½, GUILDFORD 10.

The reason for its present position is unknown.

109 CAPEL
TQ 176 411 LS II ❖

From the Epsom to Horsham turnpike of 1754 there is a cast-iron plate bolted on to a stone outside Westminster Cottage on the east side of The Street. It reads:

27 / FROM / WESTR / BRIDGE.

110 ASHTEAD
TQ 196 584 ■

Built into brick walling within the garden of Ashtead House is a milestone from the 1754 Epsom to Horsham turnpike which reads:

XVII MILES / FROM THE / STANDARD / IN / CORNHILL / LONDON / OVER THE DOWNS.

It is not certain whether this has been moved as there were road changes in this area in 1802 when the owner of Ashtead Park caused Farm Road to be moved to the east and the

east-west road through the park to be moved northwards.

111 OCKLEY
TQ 145 396 LS II ❖

This prominent milestone is outside Milestone Cottage on the west side of Stane Street. It is inscribed:

LONDON / 31 / PULBOROUGH / 15 / ARUNDEL / 24 / BOGNOR / 31.

112 HOOKWOOD
TQ 262 436 ❖

This stone on the west side of the A217 is inscribed:

LONDON 25, REIGATE $4^3/_8$, BRIGHTON 26 $^5/_8$, CRAWLEY 4 $^5/_8$.

As this milestone shows odd eighths of a mile it has been suggested that the road originally looped round to the west between Hookwood and Sidlow Bridge.

113 1930s ROAD SIGN
TQ 172 495 ❖

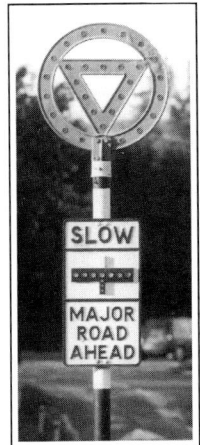

In Deepdene Drive there is still a 'SLOW–MAJOR ROAD AHEAD' sign which was put in place when the road was built before World War II. The fact that this is a private road probably explains why the sign has not been updated.

114 VANDERBILT MEMORIAL
TQ 169 456 ❖

Even after railways and buses were in operation some people still retained their private coaches. One such was the American millionaire Alfred Vanderbilt, who owned the stage coach 'The Venture' which he drove from London to the south coast, often calling at coaching inns such as *The Swan* in Leatherhead on his journey.

Vanderbilt had an affection for the road through Holmwood and following his drowning when the Lusitania sank, a granite memorial was erected by the A24 north of Bushy Croft with the following inscription:

In memory of Alfred Gwynne Vanderbilt
A gallant gentleman and fine sportsman who perished in the Lusitania May 7th 1915.
This stone erected on his favourite road by a few of his British coaching friends and admirers.

115 CARTER'S MEMORIAL

TQ 167 560   ❖

Embedded in the wall on the east of Gimcrack Hill, Leatherhead is an iron shoe which was used as a brake on horse-drawn carts by placing it under a wheel. A carter was leading his cart down the hill with the shoe on a chain under a rear wheel when the chain broke, causing the cart to run over and kill him. The iron shoe was placed in the wall as a memorial.

RAILWAYS

When the various railways in Britain were grouped into four major systems in 1923, all those in the present Mole Valley District became part of the Southern Railway. Before that, however, the London and South Western, the London Brighton and South Coast and the South Eastern and Chatham each had lines within the District.

The Reading, Guildford and Reigate company was incorporated in 1846 to build a line from Redhill to Reading and the section from Redhill (then called Reigate Junction) to Guildford was opened in 1849, becoming the first railway in what is now Mole Valley. In 1852 the line was bought by the South Eastern Railway (SER) who were keen to have a link from the channel ports to the Great Western Railway system. Following later amalgamation with the London Chatham and Dover Railway, the SER became the South Eastern and Chatham Railway (SECR).

The London and Southampton Railway opened between Nine Elms and Woking Common (later Woking) in 1838, reaching Southampton two years later, after becoming the London and South Western Railway (LSWR). Its London terminus moved to Waterloo in 1848. The station was known as Waterloo Bridge until 1886; the bridge was to be called Strand Bridge but it was renamed by an act in 1816 and opened on the second anniversary of the battle in the following year. In 1859 the branch to Leatherhead was opened. This ran from the junction where Raynes Park station was built twelve years later. The section from Epsom to Leatherhead was operated jointly with the London Brighton and South Coast Railway (LBSCR). The line terminated at a station north of the town near Kingston Road.

In 1867 the LBSCR extended the line from the Leatherhead terminus (which was then closed) to the present station and on southwards to Dorking and Horsham. At the same time the LSWR built a new terminus alongside the new LBSCR station.

The Guildford 'New' line from Hampton Court Junction to Guildford via Cobham was opened in 1885 and the connection from Effingham Junction on this line to Leatherhead via Bookham came into operation at the same time.

Following the 1923 grouping, the LSWR station at Leatherhead was closed in 1927, leaving only the old LBSCR station which remains as Leatherhead Station today. A new junction had been made south of the station enabling trains to Bookham and Effingham to use it.

The Southern Railway electrified the lines from Epsom-Leatherhead-Dorking and Leatherhead-Effingham Junction in 1925 with the section from Dorking to Horsham following in 1938.

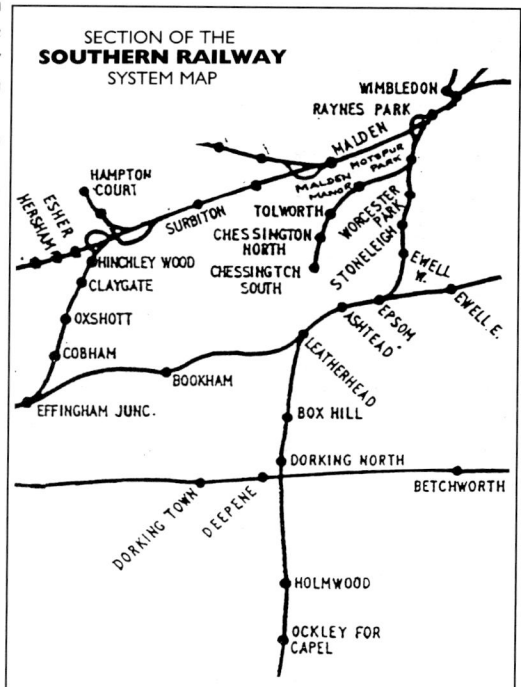

SECTION OF THE
SOUTHERN RAILWAY
SYSTEM MAP

WIMBLEDON
RAYNES PARK
MALDEN
MOTSPUR
PARK
HAMPTON COURT
ESHER
HERSHAM
MALDEN MANOR
WORCESTER PARK
SURBITON
TOLWORTH
CHESSINGTON NORTH
STONELEIGH
EWELL W.
HINCHLEY WOOD
CHESSINGTON SOUTH
CLAYGATE
EPSOM
EWELL E.
OXSHOTT
ASHTEAD
LEATHERHEAD
COBHAM
BOOKHAM
EFFINGHAM JUNC.
BOX HILL
DORKING NORTH
BETCHWORTH
DORKING TOWN
DEEPENE
HOLMWOOD
OCKLEY FOR CAPEL

116: Dorking Town
Station,1959

Photo: John Faulkner

GUILDFORD-READING LINE
116 DORKING WEST STATION
TQ 160 499 ❖

Formerly Dorking, then Dorking Town, this was Dorking's first railway station, opened in 1849. Today the station consists of two staggered platforms with bus-stop type shelters and a subway, but up to 1969 this was a substantial station with a two-storey building on the down side. There were also considerable goods sidings serving, but having no rail connection to, the adjacent timber yard and gas works as well as other local industries. Sidings on the up side were paid for by Thomas Cubitt when he was building his mansion 'Denbies' in 1850-51.

The goods shed still exists, but has no connection with the railway. The *South Eastern Railway Hotel* now *The Pilgrim* and a row of railwaymen's houses also survive.

117 DORKING (DEEPDENE)
STATION
TQ 170 501 ❖

This, Dorking's second station, was opened in 1851 as 'Box Hill and Leatherhead Road'. It was renamed 'Box Hill' and then 'Deepdene' before acquiring its present name in 1987.

The station never had goods facilities and its platforms and buildings were of wooden construction. The buildings were demolished in 1969 and replaced by bus-stop type shelters.

Trains from Reading to Gatwick Airport stop at Dorking (Deepdene)–the only stop between Guildford and Reigate–and possibly this is the reason that the station was refurbished in the early 1990s. This comprised new woodwork and paint but no facilities other than the
26 bus-stop shelters.

118 BETCHWORTH STATION
TQ 210 513 ❖

This was called 'Betchworth and Box Hill' when first opened and gained its present name when the new station down the line opened two years later. The buildings on the down side are the original 1849 structures in the steeply-gabled style found elsewhere on this line. There were at one time two signal boxes but both closed in 1934 when signal and level crossing operation was transferred to the booking office. This arrangement continued until 1983 when CCTV operation of the crossing was installed, controlled from Reigate; automatic barriers had replaced the traditional gates in 1977.

The station buildings remain but are no longer used for railway purposes, passengers now being provided with bus-stop type shelters.

There was a siding and coal yard south of the station whilst on the north side there were

118: Former Station Hotel, Betchworth
Photo: Chris Shepheard

118: Ground frame at Betchworth Station

Photo: Chris Shepheard

sidings serving the adjacent lime works, which had its own extensive rail network with three different gauges.

The ground frame at the end of the down platform which controlled access to the sidings is still in place as is the head shunt on the up side.

The house in the station forecourt, *The Beeches* was originally *Beeches Inn*, built as a station hotel, but it became a private residence in the early 20th century.

LEVEL CROSSINGS

A number of crossings, as well as that at Betchworth, existed on this stretch of line; those with manned gates were at:-

119 Hackhurst Lane TQ 097 481 ❖

120 Westcott TQ 132 495 ❖

121 Milton TQ 146 499 ❖

122 Brockham TQ 197 505 ❖

123 Buckland TQ 219 516 ❖

All the gated crossings had cottages for the crossing keepers but only the Buckland one remains, and this is no longer used by the railway. When control of the gates was established from Reigate in 1983, automatic half barriers were installed at Brockham and Buckland.

OTHER FEATURES
124 EVELYN'S SIDING
TQ 114 483 ■

Traces of this siding still exist on the up side just beyond White Down Lane. It was constructed to serve the lime works at Abinger. No trace remains of the signal box which controlled it.

125 RIFLE RANGE HALT
TQ 126 492

In 1916 military rifle ranges were built north of the railway at Coomb Farm and a halt was built here purely for the troops visiting the ranges. The station was demolished in 1928 but remains of the butts may be seen at TQ 126 494.

126 TRIPLE-ARCH SKEW BRIDGE
TQ 172 502 ❖

Just to the east of Dorking (Deepdene) station the SER crosses a footpath on a triple-arch skew bridge. The reason for the presence of such a large and expensive bridge over a

120: Hole Hill Crossing, Westcott

131: L & S W R Station, Leatherhead

Photo: Surrey Record Office

footpath is that the proposed Direct London and Portsmouth Railway (DL&PR), which was never in fact constructed, was intended to pass beneath the SER line. It would have taken a similar route to the present line from Leatherhead to Dorking, then run through the arch, turned west to join the Guildford line west of the present A24, and followed the Guildford and Reading route to Shalford.

127 BROCKHAM SIDINGS
TQ 200 506

Sidings left the north side of the railway to serve limeworks, brickworks, hearthstone mines and sand pits. The arch under the line by Pilgrim's Cottages took the siding to the sand pits.

128 BUCKLAND SIDING
TQ 236 512

This siding was on the north of the line to serve the tile works in Cliftons Lane as well as the 2' 0" gauge line to the Buckland sand pits which went under the main line through a brick arch which still exists.

EPSOM - EFFINGHAM JUNCTION AND HORSHAM
129 ASHTEAD STATION
TQ 180 590   ❖

Originally a joint LSWR/LBSCR station opened in 1859. The present buildings, which date from 1967/8, comprise a ticket office on the down side and a shelter and waiting room on the up platform.

The level crossing at the London end provides the only vehicular access to the northern part of the village. The automatic barriers are now

28 operated by closed circuit television from

Wimbledon. Previously the crossing was controlled from an adjacent signal box which was closed in 1978 and demolished the following year. This box replaced an earlier one on the up platform from which it would have been difficult to see the road.

Goods sidings were on the down side where the present car park is situated.

LEATHERHEAD STATIONS
130 TQ 165 576
131 TQ 163 568   LS II ❖

The first station in Leatherhead had been the terminus of the joint LBSCR/LSWR line from Epsom built in 1859. This stood on the east side of Kingston Road (**TQ 165 576**). The station closed when the line was extended to Dorking in 1867 and was demolished. The original engine shed survived until the 1980s. When it was relinquished by the railway it was first used as a church and a school, and latterly as a car repair depot.

The attractive LBSCR station (**TQ 163 568**) was built when the line from London to Leatherhead was extended to Dorking in 1867. The polychrome brick station with carved stone details and decorative woodwork remains almost unaltered, although the goods shed and signal boxes have disappeared except for the LBSCR signal box on the down platform, which is no longer manned.

The adjacent LSWR station was built as a terminus in 1867, but the line was extended to Bookham and Effingham Junction at the same time as the Guildford 'New' line, via Cobham, was constructed in 1885. Following the

131: Leatherhead Station   Photo: Chris Shepheard

formation of the Southern Railway, the layout south of Leatherhead was altered to avoid the use of two separate stations. A new bridge was erected over Station Road for the Effingham line and the ex-LSWR station was closed in 1927 and demolished in 1932, leaving the ex-LBSCR station to serve all lines. The bridge over Randalls Road remained until the 1970s and traces of the down side staircase may be seen in Station Road. To the west of the station site Old Station Approach remains together with 'Railway Cottages'.

132 BOOKHAM STATION
TQ 127 556 LS II   ❖

This 1885 station is in the 'Claygate' style of the New Guildford line project. The brick and tiled station has timber and corrugated sheet steel canopies, integral station master's house and a cast and wrought iron footbridge (**LS II**).

The goods yard closed in 1965 and the goods shed is now used as offices and a builder's depot.

On the London side of the station the line passes through a 91 yard long tunnel (**LS II**) which has brick portals with stone dressings; 200 yards west of the station is a road bridge (**LS II**).

133 BOXHILL AND WESTHUMBLE STATION
TQ 167 518   **LS II** ❖

Although less than a mile from Dorking, the landowner, Thomas Grissell of Norbury Park, a retired railway contractor, insisted on having his own station which had to be the most ornate on the line. He also insisted on the right to stop any train at the station on request.

The building was designed by Charles Driver and has steeply-pitched roofs with patterned tiles, exposed gable timbers and a pyramidal turret with ornamental ironwork. There is a large porch over the entrance to the station which is on the down side.

The station has had many names–'West Humble for Box Hill' until 1870, 'Boxhill and Burford Bridge' until 1896, 'Boxhill' until 1904, then 'Boxhill and Burford Bridge' again until 1985. It then became 'Boxhill and Westhumble' and is still listed as this in the timetables, but the station nameboards simply state 'Boxhill'.

134 DORKING STATION
TQ 171 504   ❖

This station was not as ornate as Leatherhead or Boxhill and Westhumble but it contained substantial two-storey buildings on the up side, including accommodation for the station master.

132: Bookham Station
under construction
  Photo: Leatherhead & District
    Local History Society

29

133: Boxhill & Westhumble Station
Drawing by Rowena Oliver

135: Holmwood Station and Signal Box
Photo: Chris Shepheard

In 1982 the up side was redeveloped with a new office block and in 1986 the remaining original buildings on the island platform were removed and replaced by a steel and glass structure.

The goods yard and engine shed have gone to make way for a car park but some carriage sidings remain, as does the typical Southern Railway 'Odeon' style signal box built in 1938.

When the LBSCR and the SECR amalgamated in 1923 with the formation of the Southern Railway this station was renamed 'Dorking North' to distinguish it from the other stations in the town. In 1968 it reverted to 'Dorking'.

135 HOLMWOOD STATION ❖
TQ 174 437

Holmwood station was built on an overbridge but the buildings at road level were demolished in 1986, leaving steps down from the road to each platform. The original slate-roofed wooden passenger shelter and signal box remain on the up platform; the signal box is still equipped and the semaphore signals are still in place. A similar shelter on the down platform has been demolished.

Originally there was a goods shed and coal yard on the down side, one of the items handled being gunpowder for the Schermuly works at Newdigate.

The old station master's house remains to the south of the station.

About a mile south of Holmwood there was at one time a private halt close to Wigmore House for the use of the Mortimore family who lived there.

136 OCKLEY STATION ❖
TQ 164 404

This station, once known as 'Ockley and Capel', retains the original buildings although in a dilapidated condition. The station house also remains together with former railway staff houses.

Ockley used to have considerable sidings to serve the adjacent brick and tile works and to handle milk and general agricultural products.

OTHER FEATURES
137-138 CHESSINGTON BRANCH: MOTSPUR PARK - LEATHERHEAD LINE

This branch from the Raynes Park to Epsom line at Motspur Park opened in 1939. It was originally intended to rejoin the original route north of Leatherhead. However the line was never built beyond Chessington South as the war intervened, then the Green Belt policy put an end to development south of what had become the terminus.

Although the extension to Leatherhead was never completed, remains of an embankment may be seen south of Chessington (at TQ 176 624 ❖). The connection at Leatherhead was to have been made 270 yards north-east of the Kingston Road bridge (at TQ 166 578 ❖) close to the site of the first Leatherhead station.

LEATHERHEAD RAILWAY BRIDGES
139 TQ 161 563 ❖
140 TQ 160 564   **LS II** ❖

Each of the lines leaving Leatherhead to the south crosses the Mole on a fine brick bridge. The Dorking line bridge was built in 1867 and the bridge carrying the line to Bookham in 1885. The earlier four-arch bridge is the more elaborate, with balustrading and stone details at the insistence of Thomas Grissell.

141 MICKLEHAM TUNNEL
TQ 164 542 - TQ 164 537   • ❖

When this 524 yard tunnel was bored through the hill in Norbury Park estate, a condition was laid down by the owner, Thomas Grissell, that there should be no vertical shafts and that the portals should receive architectural treatment. He also insisted that the three bridges taking the line over the Mole on his estate should be decorative.

142 BETCHWORTH TUNNEL
TQ 179 498 - TQ 181 496

This 385 yard tunnel was constructed through the western end of Betchworth Park. Its opening was delayed by falls of sand during its construction in 1867 and twenty years later the roof and walls gave way, causing the tunnel to be blocked by running sand. The repairs necessitated the closure of the tunnel for seven months.

143 SER/LBSCR CONNECTION
TQ 175 502

When the Dorking - Horsham line was built a single track link was installed from a point about 150 yards east of Dorking (Deepdene) to join the new line nearly half a mile south of Dorking station. This spur was, in fact, rarely used except for some race traffic, and the connection with the SER was severed around 1900. The rails were removed in 1926 only to be restored in 1941 to provide alternative routes for traffic in the event of bomb damage.

The connection was finally dismantled in 1946 and much of the land sold for housing; it is possible to trace some of the route of the spur. A connection from south of Dorking station to north of the Reigate line was proposed by the Southern Railway in 1924, but although some land was purchased, the scheme was dropped.

LEVEL CROSSINGS
With the exception of Ashtead station, the only crossings remaining on this section are footpaths and bridleways but houses built for railway staff remain at the following sites:

144 MICKLEHAM
TQ 165 534   ❖

The crossing box was closed in 1971 and demolished but the footpath crossing remains. The provision of this crossing was one of the conditions imposed by Thomas Grissell, as was the painting of the buildings green. The houses for railway staff remain adjacent to the crossing.

145 LODGE FARM
TQ 190 456   ❖

Here the box has been demolished and the crossing is closed even for pedestrians. However the houses built for railway staff remain.

THE METROPOLITAN RAILWAYS' JUNCTION RAILWAY
Before there were any railways in what is now Mole Valley, there were plans made in 1845 for a Metropolitan Railways' Junction Railway. Robert Stephenson was one of the engineers of the scheme which would have had a connection to the Brighton line at Red Hill station then going to Dorking, Leatherhead, Cobham, Weybridge (for the South Western main line), Egham, Colnbrook (with a branch to Datchet),

139-140: Railway Bridges at Leatherhead
Photo: Chris Shepheard

West Drayton (for the GWR), Berkhampstead (for the London and Birmingham Railway), Hertford, Harlow (for the Northern and Eastern Counties Railway) and round to Tilbury. The map showing these proposals indicates the London and Brighton Railway terminating at Epsom, but projected to Leatherhead to join the Metropolitan Railways' Junction line.

CHANNEL PORTS AND NORTHERN DIRECT RAILWAY

A proposal was made in 1907 for a north - south railway link to provide a direct connection (avoiding London) between northern and eastern main lines and the channel ports. The southern end of the line would have been at East Dorking where there would have been a junction with the SECR at Pixham, with running powers over the line to Redhill for connections to Hastings, Folkestone, Dover, Brighton, Newhaven and Eastbourne.

North of Dorking the line would have run through the Mole valley then across the Thames, making connections with the North Western, Midland, Great Northern and Great Eastern Railways on its way to Waltham Cross.

At the time there were strong local objections to a second railway between Leatherhead and Dorking and this potentially useful line avoiding the capital was never built.

146 PROPOSED STATION AT FETCHAM
TQ 146 566   ❖

In 1935 there was a proposal, which was not proceeded with, to build a station and goods yard at Fetcham, between Leatherhead and Bookham. This would have been just west of the Cobham Road railway bridge on land now occupied by Hilley Field Lane and Meadow Lane. The plans included a public house next to the recreation ground, a petrol station and a row of shops.

INLAND WATERWAYS

Although the District has a river flowing from one end to the other, it contains no navigable waterways. A number of proposals were made which, if any had been carried out, would have provided Mole Valley with some canal or navigation.

In 1664 an Act was granted to make the river Mole navigable from Reigate to the Thames, but this never took place. In 1668 a further proposal was made to make the Mole navigable but again no progress was made.

In 1798 Marshall in 'Rural Economy of the Southern Counties' suggested cutting a canal from Horsham to the river Arun and from Horsham to the chalk quarries at Betchworth, then down the Mole valley to Dorking.

Rennie, in 1810, had an even grander proposal, for the Grand Southern Canal linking the Medway to Portsmouth. This would have passed south of Mole Valley but a link with the Thames along the valley of the Mole was also suggested. In the same year Richard Pottinger proposed a navigation from Holmwood to Thames Ditton with connections to Stoke D'Abernon, Cobham and Esher.

The main project, however, was the Grand Imperial Ship Canal which would have stretched from London to Portsmouth, carrying large sea-going vessels and containing locks 300ft long and 64ft wide. Three routes were suggested in 1824 and one of these (the shortest) by Nicholas Cundy, would have cut right through Mole Valley from Leatherhead to south of Ockley. A bill was presented to parliament in 1828 but the government gave it no support and the scheme died.

AIR TRAVEL

An airport opened at Gatwick in 1930 which has grown into today's international airport but during the development boundary changes meant that although the original construction was in Surrey the whole site is now part of West Sussex and not, therefore, part of Mole Valley.

In 1911 Keith Prowse proposed running aeroplane flights from Brooklands to the area and it was suggested that a landing field be used at Cherkley Court estate. Although Leatherhead Council supported this the plan did not materialise. When Sir Alan Cobham in 1920 tried to encourage Leatherhead Council to have an airport in the town, this also failed.

In 1920, however, an airport did exist near Leatherhead at Malden Rushett (TQ 168 615 ■). It was run by Mr W G Chapman of Leatherhead Motor Works, Kingston Road, who erected a hanger which was brought from Brooklands Airfield at Weybridge. He used a DH6 aircraft powered by a 90hp Curtiss OX-5 engine to give joy rides and charter flights. Two years later Mr Chapman was seriously injured during an aerobatic display and the Leatherhead Aviation Service came to an end.

147 AVIATOR'S GRAVE, MICKLEHAM

TQ 170 533 ❖

Graham Gilmour, one of the best of the English pioneer aviators, was flying a Brooklands-built Martinsyde plane at the time of his death on 17 February 1912.

Gilmour had taken off from Brooklands about 11.00 am in his Antoinette-engined Martin Handasyde monoplane saying that he would be back within the hour. However, whilst flying over the Old Deer Park, Richmond, the machine suddenly failed and crashed in a tangled mass of wreckage, killing the pilot instantly.

It is thought that freak air conditions caused this crash as problems were encountered at other aerodromes in the area and flying was abandoned.

Graham Gilmour was buried in Mickleham churchyard in his parents' grave which is marked by a stone containing a picture of the type of plane which he was flying.

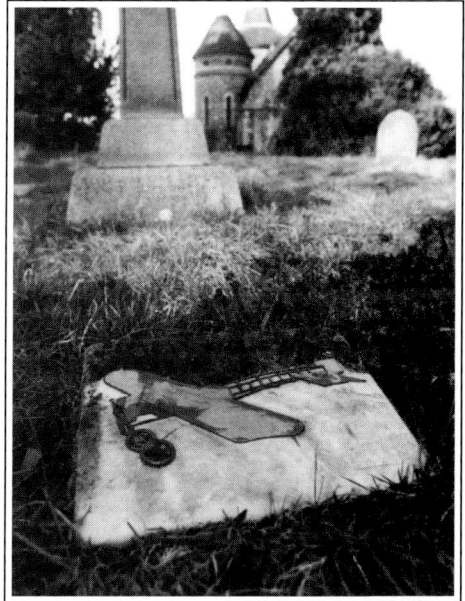

147: Aviator's Grave, Mickleham

Photo: Chris Shepheard

151: Village Pump, Brockham see page 34   *Photo: Chris Shepheard*

WATER

Before the establishment of a public water supply most places were dependent on springs or wells. Many villages had public wells and pumps, usually in a central position so that residents could easily obtain water. Although few wells are now used for supplying water there are a number of remains of machinery and/or buildings throughout the District recalling times before mains water was generally available.

148 HIGHLANDS FARM, LEATHERHEAD
TQ 185 559   **LS II** ■

The octagonal weather-boarded winding house dating from c.1808 remains beside the farmhouse, but none of the machinery survives here or in the adjacent well house.

149 BOCKETT'S FARM, FETCHAM
TQ 156 549   ❑

Here the brick-built well house is in the farmyard; although the well cover may be seen no machinery remains. The building is now used for a countryside display area by Surrey County Council; the well is beneath a model of Norbury Park.

150 TOWN PUMP, DORKING
TQ 164 493   **LSII** ❖

When the supply from the waterworks at Archway Place was insufficient for the needs of the area a former well was reopened and a pump installed. This is believed to be the pump which still exists at Pump Corner, at the junction of South Street and West Street. Until recently one of the paving slabs between the pump and the shops was marked **WELL**.

151 BROCKHAM PUMP
TQ 196 495 photo: see previous page   **LS II** ❖

This hand-operated iron pump, made by Warners of London, is protected by a tiled roof supported on wooden columns; it was erected *in memory of Henry Thomas Hope Esq. (of Deepdene) by his neighbours and tenants resident in the district of Brockham to commemorate his numerous acts of benevolence and his readiness on all occasions both to promote and support public improvement* Mr Hope died in 1862.

152 HEADLEY
TQ 203 550   ❖

The original village well remains a few yards to the south of the footpath off Church Lane. The brick structure is protected by an iron cage.

153 LEIGH PUMP
TQ 224 469   **LS II** ❖

The village pump on the green is covered by a wooden structure roofed with stone slabs which also commemorates a number of awards for the best kept village.

148: Well-house, Highlands Farm
Photo: Chris Shepheard

150: Town Pump, Dorking   *Drawing: Peter Watkins*

154 ST. JAMES' WELL, ABINGER COMMON
TQ 120 454   **LS II** ❖

This well, built by William John Evelyn, Lord of the Manor of Abinger, was declared open for the use of Abinger parishioners on 11 August 1893.

The pump operating gear is still in situ under a roof of stone slabs supported on round sandstone columns.

155 HOLMBURY ST MARY PUMP
TQ 112 443   ❖

Here the pump on the village green is protected by a thatched shelter supported on wooden columns.

156 WINDPUMP, CAPEL
TQ 170 435   ❖

Alongside the footpath from Moorhurst Road to Bognor Road there remains a Climax wind engine mounted on a lattice steel tower with a water storage tank alongside mounted on steel supports. The annular sail for the wind pump lies on the ground at the base of the support tower.

Climax wind engines were made by Thomas and Son of Worcester.

157 FOREST GREEN
TQ 121 412   ❖

Outside the house known as 'The Old Post Office', the handle and linkage from a water pump remain next to the front door.

158 BRITTLEWARE FARM, CHARLWOOD
TQ 245 432   **LS II** ■

In the garden of Brittleware Farm there is an example of a private pump surrounded by a wooden casing.

159 CHARLWOOD PUMP
TQ 241 411   ❖

The village pump stands in the churchyard wall near the gate by the Half Moon public house. The machinery is housed within the stonework but the spout and handle have disappeared since the 1950s. The pump became redundant when mains water came to Charlwood in 1896

160 OCKLEY
TQ 147 402   **LS II** ❖

On Ockley Green there is an oak-framed canopy of Horsham stone slabs supported by four columns. These were originally constructed from Leith Hill stone but following damage by a car in 1985 they were all replaced.

The pump was given to the village by Miss Jane Scott in 1837. No machinery remains above ground. Beneath a seat on a stone slab is a 70ft deep well from which water used to be drawn by an iron pump which was in position until September 1965.

Most of the pump machinery is believed to survive and, together with the canopy, is in the care of Ockley parish council.

156: Wind Pump, Capel   *Photo: Chris Shepheard*   **35**

MOLE VALLEY DISTRICT

FOR DETAIL MAPS OF LEATHERHEAD AND DORKING
SEE PAGE 72

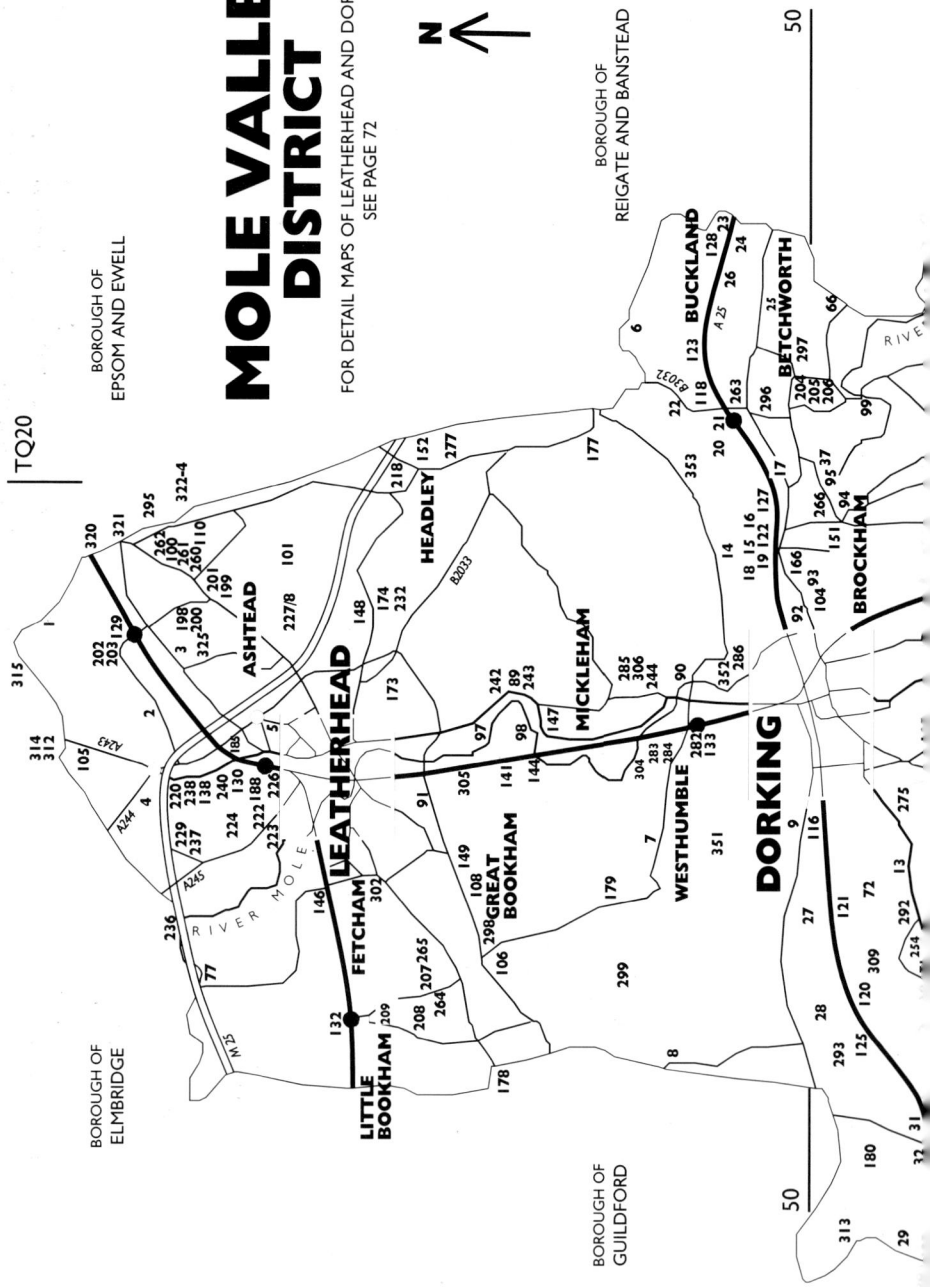

N

BOROUGH OF
EPSOM AND EWELL

BOROUGH OF
REIGATE AND BANSTEAD

BOROUGH OF
ELMBRIDGE

BOROUGH OF
GUILDFORD

LEATHERHEAD

FETCHAM

LITTLE
BOOKHAM

GREAT
BOOKHAM

ASHTEAD

HEADLEY

MICKLEHAM

WESTHUMBLE

DORKING

BUCKLAND

BETCHWORTH

BROCKHAM

RIVER MOLE

RIVER

M25

A24

A243

A244

A245

A25

B2033

B2032

315
320
321
295
322-4
314
312
105
202 129
203
2
1
236
77
146
132
209
208 264 265
207
178
106
298
108
149
179
299
8
3 198 200
325
262 100
261
260 110
201 199
101
227/8
148
174 232
152 277
218
173
297
242
89
243
98
147
97
141
144
305
91
7
351
299
285
306
244
90
283
284
282
133
352
286
9
116
27
121
72
13
292
254
275
28
120 309
125
293
180
313
29
32 31
277
177
353
14
18 15 16
19 122 127
92
104 93
166
151 94
266
17
296
204 297
205 206
99
37
95
66
123
128 23
24
26
25
263
118
22
20 21
302
224
237
229
238
138
240
220
222 188 226
223
130
18/
5/

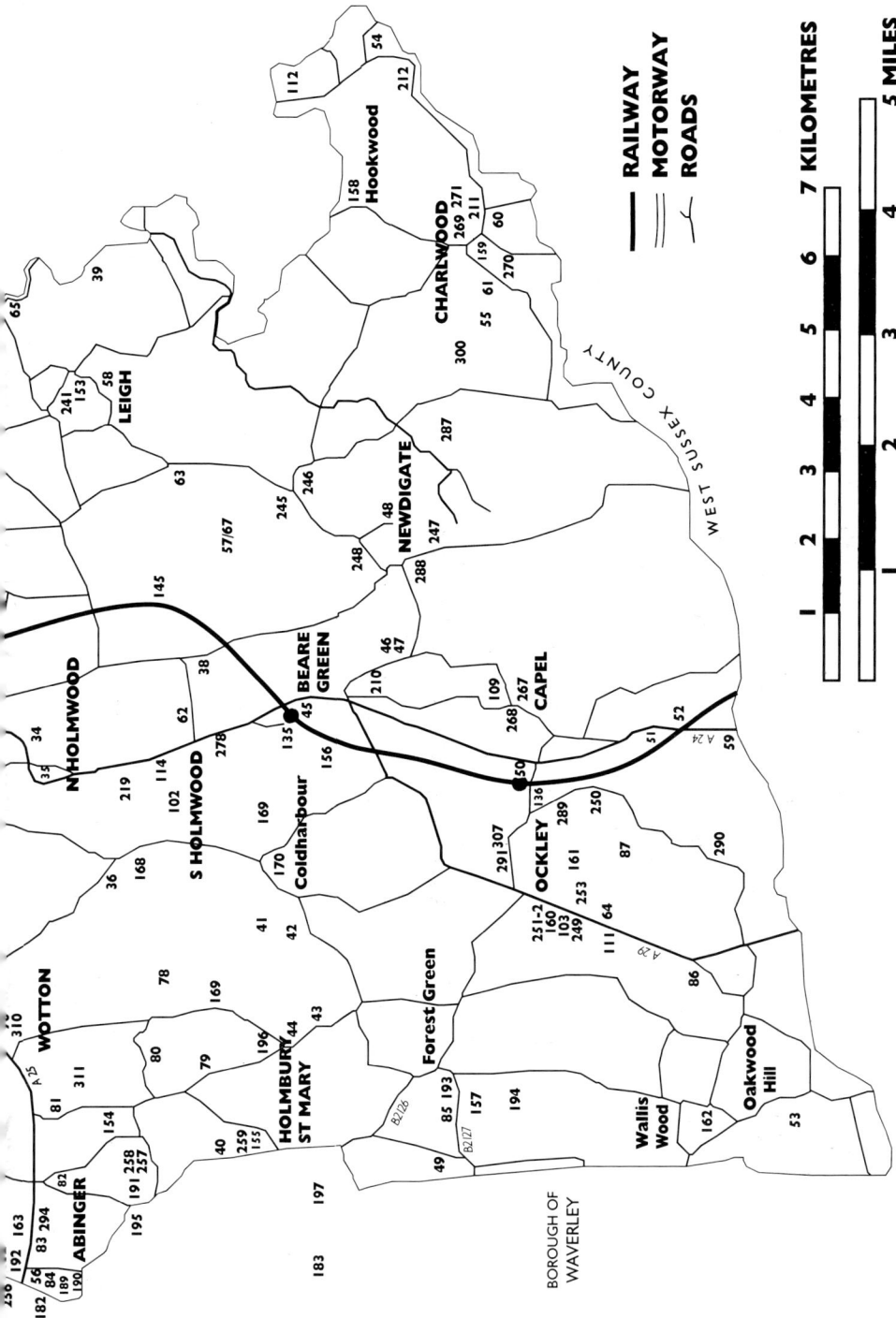

RAILWAY
MOTORWAY
ROADS

7 KILOMETRES
5 MILES

65

39

112
54

Hookwood
158
212

CHARLWOOD
269 271
211
60
159
61 270
55
300

LEIGH
241 153
58

63

57/67
245
246

NEWDIGATE
48
247
287

248
288

145

N HOLMWOOD
34
35
38
62
114
219
102

BEARE GREEN
45
135
156
278

46
47
210
109
268 267
CAPEL
50

WEST SUSSEX COUNTY

51
52
A 24
55

Coldharbour
169
170
41
42

OCKLEY
136
289
250
291 307
253 161
160 251-2
103
249
111 64
87
290

86
A 28

168
36

WOTTON
310
311
81
78
80
79
154
40 259 155
82
191 258 257
195

A 25

HOLMBURY ST MARY
196
44
43

Forest Green
B 2126
85 193
B 2127
157
194
49

ABINGER
156 192 163
56
83 294
84
189
190
182

197

183

Wallis Wood
162

Oakwood Hill
53

BOROUGH OF WAVERLEY

I 1 2 3 4 5 6

1 2 3 4

164: Sign on Dorking's first Waterworks, Archway Place
Photo: Chris Shepheard

161 VANN FARM
TQ 153 401

During part of the 19th century water for Vann House was pumped from a well in this field north of the farm. The well-head machinery, manufactured by Warner and Co of London, is still in place.

162 WALLISWOOD PUMP
TQ 119 382   **LS II** ❖

Here, on the village green, the well is covered by a tiled canopy supported on round sandstone columns. The well-head machinery by Warners is still in position.

163 PRIVATE WATER SUPPLY, ABINGER HALL
TQ 105 475   ■

Abinger Hall had its own water supply system which. although the main house was demolished in 1959, still remains in operation to serve properties around the stable yard.

In a pumphouse near the Tillingbourne there is a three-throw pump driven by an 11ft diameter undershot waterwheel. The water is pumped about 150ft from a nearby circular brick-lined well about 30ft deep with a bore-hole of about 40ft below that, to a 30,000 gallon reservoir from which it feeds to about half a dozen properties.

There has been a water-driven pump on this site since at least 1803. The waterwheel is believed to be the original one and the present pump was installed in 1872 and thoroughly overhauled in 1992. The pumphouse was demolished in the storm of 1987, but miraculously the pump survived and continued working until the house was rebuilt.

WATER SUPPLY COMPANIES
164-171 DORKING AREA

The first public water supply to Dorking was from a pumping station at Archway Place, off Church Street adjoining the Pippbrook (TQ 164 496 ■). This building still exists as 'Brookside' and carries an iron plate inscribed **R P Waterworks, erected 1738**. The initials refer to Resta Patching, a Dorking Quaker, who was one of the founders of the company.

Water from a spring was pumped by water-driven engines powered by the Pippbrook and distributed through bored tree trunks and later cast-iron pipes to the town centre. Eventually the spring became polluted and the works closed in the middle of the 19th century. Two cottages in Archway Place were the old waterworks cottages.

In 1869 the Dorking Water Company was incorporated; they built a 300ft deep well and steam-driven pumphouse at Harrow Road East together with a reservoir at Tower Hill. The waterworks building was sold in 1919 and converted to private dwellings (TQ 168 485 ■) and the reservoir still feeds the Dorking area.

The company also supplied the Westcott area from springs in Redlands Wood, the Rookery and Mag's Well.

Water for the town was insufficient and the company sank a borehole at Castle Gardens to augment the supply to Tower Hill. The pumphouse was near the sawmill for the Deepdene estate and remains of some of the pipework still exist in gardens of houses in Castle Gardens (TQ 188 503 ■) close to the water wheel. They also arranged for bulk supplies from the East Surrey Water Company, which were never used.

170: Water Tank, Coldharbour *Photo: Chris Shepheard*

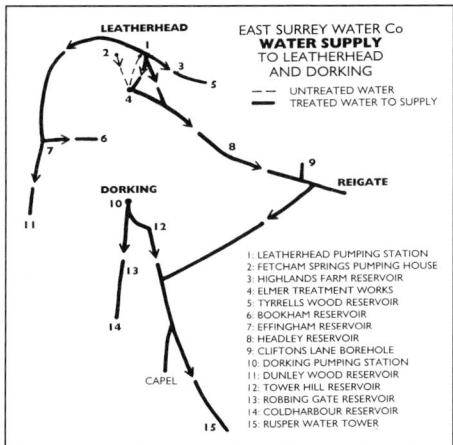

EAST SURREY WATER Co
WATER SUPPLY
TO LEATHERHEAD
AND DORKING

– – UNTREATED WATER
▬▬ TREATED WATER TO SUPPLY

LEATHERHEAD

DORKING

REIGATE

CAPEL

1: LEATHERHEAD PUMPING STATION
2: FETCHAM SPRINGS PUMPING HOUSE
3: HIGHLANDS FARM RESERVOIR
4: ELMER TREATMENT WORKS
5: TYRRELLS WOOD RESERVOIR
6: BOOKHAM RESERVOIR
7: EFFINGHAM RESERVOIR
8: HEADLEY RESERVOIR
9: CLIFTONS LANE BOREHOLE
10: DORKING PUMPING STATION
11: DUNLEY WOOD RESERVOIR
12: TOWER HILL RESERVOIR
13: ROBBING GATE RESERVOIR
14: COLDHARBOUR RESERVOIR
15: RUSPER WATER TOWER

The site of the next pumping station in Station Road (TQ 162 495 ■) was purchased in 1902 and the steam-driven equipment by Warners Ltd was pumping water from three artesian wells alongside the station by 1904. Worthington Simpsom steam pumps were installed at Station Road in 1913, 1927 and 1934 whilst the spring supplies were closed down from the Rookery (1915), Redlands (1932) and Mag's Well (1938) following the installation of further bores and mains, as well as the construction of reservoirs at Robbing Gate (TQ 157 460 ■) and Coldharbour. near Anstiebury Camp (TQ 135 440 ■)

The Coldharbour reservoir, which was opened in 1948, had been built by German prisoners of war. Following this the water tank in Coldharbour (TQ 151 440 ❖) went out of use. This covered reservoir built into the green outside the Plough Inn remains; villagers used to collect water from a tap at the side.

In 1965 the East Surrey Water Company (who had taken over the Dorking company in 1959) built a new pumping station in Beech Close (TQ 159 495 ■) equipped with automatically operated electrically-driven pumps and standby diesel generators. This replaces the works in Station Road; however, the building survives and is used by Knight Bros.

172-180 LEATHERHEAD AREA

The Leatherhead and District Waterworks Company opened its works between Waterway Road and Bridge Street (TQ 162 563 ■) in 1884, where a borehole was sunk and the pumphouse built to supply water to a reservoir towards the top of Reigate Road. This reservoir, which has been disused since 1935, may be reached from a footpath off Windmill Drive which runs behind Yarm Court Road (TQ 173 555 ■). Adjacent to the reservoir is a dilapidated wooden building containing a pressure vessel and some pipework.

The pumping station contained two 30hp steam-driven pumps to lift the water the 210 feet to the reservoir. The undertaking supplied water to the parishes of Leatherhead, Mickleham, Ashtead, the Bookhams, Fetcham, Stoke D'Abernon and Cobham.

below: 172: Leatherhead Pumping Station
Drawing: Peter Watkins

172: Demolition of Leatherheads first Pumping Station *Photo: Leatherhead & District Local History Society*

After ten years the first engine was replaced. The second followed three years later in 1897, at the same time as a larger reservoir was commissioned opposite Highlands Farm (TQ 183 558 ■). In 1909 this was enlarged and it remains the service reservoir for the area. This new reservoir had an electrical remote-indicating system to the pumphouse which was one of the first to be installed.

Further engines and pumps were added in the pumphouse in 1905 and 1912, and by 1918 the first two replacement engines were scrapped.

When additional pump capacity was needed in 1927 a diesel-driven unit was installed. Additional boreholes were sunk in 1898, 1903, 1907, 1910, and 1924 as the demand for water rose, although only the 1924 ones remain in use.

The East Surrey Water Company (ESWC), which had started as the Caterham Spring Water Company in 1862, took over the Leatherhead Company in 1927.

In 1935 a second pumping station was built in reinforced concrete adjacent to the earlier one; this was extended in 1940 and still remains. The system was modernised in 1984 by the installation of electrically-driven pumps and emergency diesel generators. The original brick-built pumphouse was demolished in 1992 and the site has been developed for housing.

The ESWC, unlike the Leatherhead company, always softened its water and in 1935 built the Elmer treatment works on Hawkshill (TQ 159 557 ■). All the water from the pumping station boreholes and from later ones sunk between the treatment works and Young Street (a total of 12 million gallons a day) is pumped to the Elmer works for treatment before being pumped to supply.

Since 1962, after their purchase of the millpond in Fetcham in 1958, the ESWC has been allowed to take up to 3 million gallons a day from ten artesian wells that feed the pond, provided that they keep the mill pond full. This water is pumped to the Elmer works by the electrically operated Fetcham Springs pumphouse (TQ 157 561 ■).

As the sources of water have been increased the Elmer treatment works has been enlarged and modernised.

The first works used Clark's process in which quicklime was mixed with water in tanks where it was agitated by compressed air until it had dissolved. After settling this produced sludge at the bottom of the tank and clear 'lime water' above. The lime water was transferred to a larger softening tank where it was mixed with hard water from the boreholes. The lime caused chalk to form and settle leaving softened water above.

In 1964 a second works, the Permutit works, was built on the site to deal with the water from Fetcham springs. This also used lime, but in a continuous process. The lime was mixed with water in a conical vessel stirred by a paddle. The sludge settled in an adjacent vessel allowing the clear lime water to be decanted from the top. In a similar vessel the lime water was added to the water from the boreholes.

By 1985 it was necessary to increase the capacity of the works and a new automated system was installed to replace both older works, although much of the Permutit equipment survives. Now the incoming water is first aerated and then treated with lime in vessels where the chalk is removed by being deposited on fine sand. After filtration the water is chlorinated before flowing into two independent pumping stations. One, constructed in 1988, is located on the Elmer site and pumps water to a reservoir, extended in 1991, at Headley (TQ 207 527 ■) which supplies the Redhill, Reigate and Salfords areas. The other pumping to supply takes place in the Bridge Street works which pumps water to reservoirs on either side of the Mole: Highlands Farm to the east or Effingham (TQ 119 527 ■) to the west. Linked to these are smaller reservoirs at Bookham (TQ 145 526 ■), Tyrells Wood (TQ 193 553 ■) and Dunley Wood (TQ 112 490 ■), a borehole in Clifton's Lane, Buckland and water towers at Rusper (TQ 204 382 ■),

pumped to supply.

Betchworth and Margery.

181-183 ABINGER, HOLMBURY ST MARY, OCKLEY ETC.

In 1890 the Shere Manor Water Company built a pumphouse by the Tillingbourne in Lower Road, Shere (TQ 072 478 ■) operated by a waterwheel. By c1900 this plant had been taken over as a sewage pumphouse. Although this operation has ceased, the building remains as a private residence called 'The Old Pumphouse'.

After a few years wells were sunk at 'High House' further upstream and a turbine driven by the Tillingbourne was used to pump water for the area as well as to generate electricity for the Manor House.

The Hurtwood Water Company installed pumps driven by a waterwheel in Netley Mill (TQ 079 479 ■) in 1903. An oil engine was installed in 1912, and other engines were added later. However, a steel overshot wheel was still used to drive a water pump until the middle of the 20th century.

Following the takeover of the Hurtwood company by the Guildford and Godalming Water Board in 1952 the source was developed and a new pumping station built adjacent to Netley Mill. The old mill and headquarters of the Hurtwood company were then sold for conversion to a private residence and the mill pond was restored.

In 1966 the G&GWB was absorbed into the West Surrey Water Board which in turn passed into the Thames Water Authority in 1974, becoming Thames Water Utilities on privatisation in 1989.

All the water for the parts of Mole Valley District which are not supplied by the East Surrey company is pumped from Netley to a service reservoir on Hurtwood Common (TQ 094 437 ■), whence it gravitates to Holmbury, Abinger, Wotton and other villages. Supplies for the higher properties are boosted by small pumping stations at Holmbury and Abinger.

GAS

184 DORKING
TQ 160 497   ■

The Gas works in Station Road was built in 1834 by the Dorking Gas Light Company to provide street lighting for the town. The works was extended in 1882, 1896 and again in 1902 when a large gasholder was erected. Land at the western end of the site was obtained in 1930 and what is now the only gas holder remaining on the site was built here in 1951.

The company merged with the Redhill company in 1928 to become the East Surrey Gas Company and their mains were interconnected.

In 1937 the gas company bought the adjacent timber yard of Taylor and Brooker but, in fact, the works was not extended and this land was used only for coke storage. Like the timber yard the gas works had no rail connection to the neighbouring sidings at Dorking Town station and the coal was transported the short distance by horse and cart and later by lorry.

Coal gas production ceased in October 1956 and the surviving holder stores North Sea gas. The remaining buildings were demolished and the site converted into a business park.

185 LEATHERHEAD
TQ 165 575

The works in Kingston Road was opened by

184: Gasholder at Dorking   *Photo: Chris Shepheard*

the Leatherhead Gas and Lighting Company in 1851 close to the site of the future railway station. Coal was initially delivered by road from Epsom until the railway arrived in 1859.

In 1906 a siding was built from the LBSCR **41**

goods yard to the opposite side of Kingston Road to serve the gas works and the Faldo Asphalte Company.

Vertical retorts were installed in 1922 and an oil/gas plant in 1927.

The company had purchased the Cobham Gas Light and Coke Company in 1912 and was itself taken over by the Wandsworth Gas Company in 1936 when its mains were connected into their system, allowing gas making at Leatherhead to cease in 1938 and the retort houses to be dismantled.

After conversion of supplies to natural gas in 1971 only two of the original four holders remained in service but these were dismantled in the 1980s.

Some of the gas works buildings are now used by a plant hire company.

ELECTRICITY

186 DORKING
TQ 162 496 ■

In 1903 Dorking Urban District Council financed the erection of the power station in Station Road which was built by Edmundson's Electricty Corporation who leased it from the council.

The original plant consisted of two 90kW steam-driven DC generators which were augmented by a 200kW steam set in 1915 and two 200kW diesel-driven generators in 1928.

Initially the supply was confined to the town centre but in 1913 it was extended to include Westcott. In 1928 further extensions covered Betchworth, Buckland, Leigh, Newdigate, Capel, Forest Green, Oakwood Hill, Holmbury St Mary, Abinger and Wotton.

In 1931 the Edmundson's installation was taken over by the London and Home Counties Joint Electricity Authority (JEA) who established a bulk supply point at Dorking power station allowing alternating current to be available for the first time, although the last DC consumer was not converted until 1957.

The power station building remains together with the adjacent house in which the engineer lived. One of the early electric street lamps is still mounted on a bracket on the corner of the building.

187 LEATHERHEAD
TQ 162 562

Leatherhead's power station was built in 1902 by the Leatherhead and District Electricity Company Ltd. It was situated just downstream of the town bridge by the waterworks.

The works contained a 75kW diesel-driven generator with lead-acid batteries to absorb peak loads. This DC supply was initially to Leatherhead only but it was soon extended to Ashtead, Mickleham and Fetcham. In 1913 the company obtained an order to supply AC to Cobham, Stoke D'Abernon, the Bookhams and Effingham; in 1925 this was extended to East and West Horsley, East Clandon and part of Chessington and by 1927 Headley was included. By 1920 the works contained 5 diesel-driven generators with a total installed capacity of 710 kW.

In 1925 a new works was built above the bridge, on the site still occupied by Seeboard, containing a 500kW alternator driven by a Fullager diesel engine. The generator control panel for this set was in the switchboard of the old engine room on the opposite side of the main road. By 1928 the demand had increased so much that a further generator was needed and the first 1000kW Fullager set to be installed in the British Isles was added to the new works. At the same time the new switchboard was erected in the new engine room.

186: Power Station with Lamp, Dorking

187: Advertisement for Electricity in Leatherhead
S E D Fortescue Collection

The undertaking was absorbed by the London and Home Counties JEA in 1930 when a bulk supply point was established, fed from Croydon via Epsom.

The original plant was scrapped in 1934 and the building demolished leaving the site wholly occupied by the waterworks; the remaining 1500kW alternators were surplus to requirements by 1939.

DC consumers remained in the town centre until the last one was disconnected by the Chairman of Leatherhead UDC on 25 January 1961.

Some examples of old cast-iron distribution cabinets, probably used for street lighting control, may be seen at the south-east junction of Cobham Road and Lower Road (**TQ 155 561**) and in the centre of the Plough roundabout (**TQ 165 573**). These are embossed **SIEMENS 1880 LONDON**.

Another larger cabinet stands on the west side of Manor House Lane, Little Bookham. This has a plate fixed to it indicating that it belonged to the L&HCJEA, Leatherhead. It was cast by Hardy Padmore of Worcester.

SUPPLIES FROM THE NATIONAL GRID

The scheme for the transmission system for South Eastern England was outlined in the Electricity (Supply) Act, 1926. This entailed the provision of bulk supplies at 33kV to Epsom, Dorking, Reigate and Leatherhead from Croydon Power Station.

By 1930 an arrangement was in place to supply the JEA from Croydon Corporation to Epsom, and by the end of the year the JEA took supplies at Leatherhead. By 1931 much of the secondary (33kV) transmission system of the Central Electricity Board in South Eastern England had been completed including the 33kV ring from Epsom via Leatherhead, Dorking and Reigate back to Epsom.

Most of this original installation in Mole Valley still exists comprising steel-cored aluminium conductors supported on lattice steel towers. Parts of the overhead line system which may be easily seen are at Ashtead Common **TQ 191 597 ❖**), Westhumble (**TQ 156 527** to **162 503 ❖**), Box Hill (**TQ 178 506** to **199 508 ❖**) and Buckland (**TQ 238 512** to **214 524 ❖**).

The initial transformer installations at Dorking and Leatherhead were two 1kVA, 33/11k and two 3kVA, 33/6.6kV respectively. Substations still exist in the original positions adjacent to the sites of the power stations.

Later modifications have been made to the original CEB 33kV system in the area to include sub-stations at Buckland, Colley Lane and Effingham.

188 LEATHERHEAD GRID SUBSTATION ■
TQ 163 573

The 132kV grid system as originally planned for South Eastern England was completed in 1933. In 1935 it was decided to provide a feed to the 33kV Epsom Ring in addition to that from Croydon by establishing a 132kV transforming station at Leatherhead adjacent to the railway, west of Kingston Road.

This substation was connected into the existing 132kV line from Woking to Wimbledon, feeding the 33kV system by underground cables to the old power station site.

The 132kV overhead lines may be seen in the north of the District between **TQ 160 577** and **TQ 152 589** and then to **TQ 147 590** and **TQ 162 600** en route to West Weybridge and Chessington respectively.

The line terminating near Dorincourt in Oaklawn Road is an experimental line built for the Central Electricity Research Laboratories.

The main industries in Mole Valley District, other than farming and forestry, have been dealt with in the previous chapters. This chapter gives examples of some of the other industrial activities which have taken place; they are listed on a parish or locality basis.

ABINGER
189-190 WATERCRESS GROWING
TQ 098 473   ■

The mill pond at Abinger Hammer covered about three acres upstream of the bay through which the Tillingbourne now flows. Between the bay of Paddington Pond and the Abinger bay William Smith began to grow watercress in the sandy soil and spring water about 1850.

The business was taken over by Richard and John Coe, of the Shere tanning family, and by 1888 they had 25 acres of watercress beds extending down to Chilworth. They employed up to 30 people producing an annual output of 400 tons, most of which was despatched by rail from Gomshall.

The spring water feeding the beds is kept separate from the stream, some being piped under the Green to feed the beds to the west.

The Coes built eight cottages (now Fern Cottages) which had rooms at the back in which watercress was packed into baskets.

This was the first large-scale watercress growing business in the country and in 1995 it is still operated by the same family. Some of the beds downstream of the present growing area (at TQ 092 475 ■) have been re-used as a trout farm.

191 SUTTON FORGE
TQ 104 459   ■

Collinsons were blacksmiths in Sutton Abinger until 1913 when the business was taken over by Mr Etherington who operated here until the

1920s. Etheringtons also ran a smith and farrier business in Abinger Hammer (TQ 095 475 ■) in a building which became a garage and then in the 1930s a tea room known as 'Grim's Kitchen', which closed around 1970.

The 17th century cottage at Sutton remains with the smithy apparently converted to a garage.

192 ABINGER HAMMER FORGE
TQ 097 474

A blacksmith had operated on the site of Clock House since the 17th century. Before Clock House was built in 1891 the smithy moved a short distance to the east where it still carries on today.

193 FOREST GREEN FORGE
TQ 122 413

A forge has operated here for at least 200 years, at one time it was worked by the same blacksmith as those at Ockley and Oakwood Hill. The original bellows were used until 1988 when electricity was introduced into the workshop.

The present business still carries out repairs and refurbishment but it concentrates on making artistic hand-forged wrought iron work.

In 1994 the owner, James Davies, had a 16th century barn erected on the end of the smithy. This barn came from Andrew's Farm in Warnham. It is used as a museum and gallery showing old tools as well as examples of work made in the forge.

194 FOREST GREEN WHEELWRIGHT
TQ 123 407

Albert Farley was a carpenter and wheelwright for many years in New Road. His premises have now disappeared but a tyring platform remains in the driveway to one of the houses.

195 LAVENDER GROWING AND DISTILLING
TQ 104 456

Woodcote Estate was built in the 1920s on lavender fields owned by the Lomax family who lived at Woodhouse Farm, where they also had a distillery.

Photo: Chris Shepheard

196 ROYAL OBSERVATORY
TQ 128 440 ■

Continuous recording of the Earth's magnetic field had taken place at the Royal Greenwich Observatory since 1847 but when the railway at Greenwich was electrified it became necessary to find a magnetically 'quiet' location. In fact the Southern Railway agreed to pay the Observatory to move the magnetic department to any site which they chose.

In 1923 the Admiralty decided to move it to a site at Abinger Bottom and from 1924 all magnetic measurements were taking place here. However, the continued electrification of the Southern Railway began to affect the work, so that, by 1937 a further move was proposed. World War II intervened and it was not until 1957 that the Magnetic Department moved to Hartland Point in North Devon, away from the magnetic interference at Abinger.

Greenwich Observatory had been providing standard time since the middle of the 19th century and the Greenwich Time Signal was first broadcast by the BBC in 1924. With the prospect of war in 1939, and the importance of the various time signals transmitted from Greenwich, it was decided to install a time system in a blast-proof building at the Magnetic Observatory at Abinger. During the World War II the time signal was generated from Abinger and Edinburgh, and after the war from Abinger and Greenwich.

Many extra staff from Greenwich were here during the war, and the offices of the Astronomer Royal were at 'Cornerways' in Sutton Abinger. When the staff returned to Greenwich after the war 'Cornerways' became a hostel for the Admiralty staff. 'Cornerways' (TQ 100 460 ■) is once again a private house, now called 'Sutton Place Farm'.

After 'Cornerways' the Admiralty Civilian Hostel was set up in 'Feldemore' in Pasture Wood Road (TQ 115 445 ■). This large private house had been requisitioned by the army during World War II. When the Admiralty moved from Abinger this house and grounds were taken over by Belmont School from Westcott.

Soon after Greenwich Observatory moved to Hurstmonceux in 1957, the time department from Abinger also moved there and the observatory here closed. Most of the site was purchased by Surrey County Council from the Admiralty in 1961. Most of the observatory

196: Boundary Marker, Abinger

Drawing: Peter Watkins

buildings were demolished but their Countryside Ranger lives in the caretaker/mechanic's quarters re-named 'The Old Observatory'. The house which was occupied by the Officer-in-Charge, is now known as 'Forest Lodge'.

The boundary of the site was marked by stones engraved with an anchor, indicating the connection with the Admiralty. At least two of these remain together with a concrete column which used to support the azimuth mark.

197 SPACE SCIENCE LABORATORY, HOLMBURY ST MARY
TQ 105 426 ■

The Mullard Space Science Laboratory is part of the Department of Space and Climate Physics of University College, London.

The space research group was formed in the early 1950s and moved to Holmbury House in 1965 with the help of a gift from the Mullard company, hence the name of the laboratory. Holmbury House, built in the 1860s, was a private house until the 1950s, when it became a school before being taken over for MSSL.

This is the largest space science research group in the country. Much of the research is based on measurements and observations taken on rocket and satellite missions.

ASHTEAD PHOTOGRAPHIC WORKS

In the latter part of the 19th century Ashtead became a small centre for photographic manufacture. Mawson & Swan's Photographic Dry Plate Works was established between **45**

Drawing: Peter Watkins

Greville Park Road and Northfields (The Greville Works) just before 1890.

In 1895 this works was taken over by James Cadett and William Neall to form Cadett & Neall. They then built Victoria Works on the north side of West Hill, and Crampshaw Works south of West Hill between Parkers Lane and Rectory Lane, completing both before 1900. One works made photographic plates and the other photographic paper. In 1903 the company was bought by Eastman Kodak who moved the operation to Harrow five years later.

198 GREVILLE WORKS

TQ 184 580

Mawson & Swan's works was taken over by Peto & Radford who had been making electrical accumulators in an old laundry in Crampshaw Lane. After World War I they moved to Dagenham. The building, in Greville Close, was converted for residential use.

199 CRAMPSHAW WORKS

TQ 184 579

Cadett & Neall's Crampshaw factory was taken over in 1926 by Brifex Ltd. who manufactured leathercloth for bus and car seats, bookbinding and passport covers.

The building was converted into offices in 1972 and W S Atkins, civil engineers, now occupies the site.

200 VICTORIA WORKS AND ASHTEAD POTTERIES

TQ 185 580

After the departure of the photographic **46** manufacturer Cadett & Neall, in 1903, the

works was occupied by P & R Storage Battery Company until 1912, when it was purchased by W Galloway and Co of Gateshead. Galloways were a long-established firm who wished to expand their business as selling agents for Stanley steam cars which were imported from Newton, Mass. in the USA. They also had a London showroom in Shaftesbury Avenue but both the Ashtead depot and the showroom were closed in 1916 due to difficulties in obtaining supplies during World War I.

Interestingly Stanley was originally in the photographic business and was bought out by Kodak before going into steam car manufacture. During World War I Victoria Works was used as an army clothing store.

In 1922 Ashtead Potters Ltd was formed to train ex-servicemen and their dependants in the manufacture of pottery. They moved into Victoria Works in 1923 with a staff of four but by 1926 they employed between 30 and 40 people on the site. A subsidiary company, Fabric Photos Ltd, was also formed with the same training objectives, but this did not last long.

The pottery initially contained two coal-fired kilns; in 1932 an oil-fired kiln was added before the earlier two were converted to oil-firing.

Although the pottery successfully fulfilled the aims of its founders, Sir Lawrence and Lady Weaver, in providing work for disabled ex-servicemen and producing saleable products, it closed in 1935 due to the depression and the death of both Weavers. The products of this venture have become collectable and a display about the works, and examples of the products may be seen at Leatherhead Museum.

Further information on the pottery may be obtained from **The Ashtead Potters Ltd. in Surrey** by Edward Hallam (1990).

In 1927 Celestion Ltd, radio engineers, occupied Victoria Works. In 1946 the Mc Murdo Instrument Company took over the building and manufactured plastic equipment such as photographic items, valve holders, plugs and sockets and model railway parts until 1964. This substantial red-brick building with three floors totalling 17,000 square feet was bought by Leatherhead Urban District Council around 1965. It was let as a shirt warehouse and then was used by Universal Car Supplies until it was demolished in 1985.

A home for the elderly, Limetree Court, which has been built on the site, has a commemorative plaque about the potteries in the entrance.

201 POTTERY WORKERS' HOUSING, PURCELL CLOSE
TQ 189 581 ■

The Ashtead Potters Housing Society was registered in 1925 'to build 20 sound and delightful cottages around a village green – a little paradise for twenty of the workers who had no homes'.

Plaques erected on the green at Purcell Close read:

Enshrines for ever the name of one who loved and served them well. Kathleen Purcell, Lady Weaver, 18 January 1927.

In 1925 these homes were built by Ashtead Potters Housing Society for which Kathleen Purcell, Lady Weaver, collected a gift fund of £5310.

In 1929 a mortgage of £6071 was paid off by the trustees of the Douglas Haig Memorial Homes. Purcell Close is now held by them for the benefit of ex-servicemen for ever.

So, although Ashtead Pottery has disappeared, their workers' housing still remains, and is still lived in by disabled ex-servicemen.

202 TEA GARDENS
TQ 179 590 ■

One 'industry' which thrived in Ashtead before World War II was catering for large parties, mainly of children, who came from towns to enjoy themselves in the open air on Ashtead Common.

There were large refreshment huts near the station on both sides of the railway together

201: Purcell Close, Ashtead   *Photo: Chris Shepheard*

with roundabouts, helter-skelters and swings. One, the Rosary Tea Gardens, advertised as 'Caterers for School Treats, Picnics and Pleasure Parties'.

All had closed by the outbreak of war and only one of the buildings, north of the station, survives. This is now used by an engineering company.

203 LEATHER WORKS
TQ 179 589

The Rosary Leather Works, known locally as 'The Skin Factory', was owned by Swabey & Saunders. It was situated south of the railway on what is now Woodfield Close. The works operated between 1911 and 1922 and had its own gas-making plant.

BETCHWORTH
204 FORGE
TQ 211 497 **LS II**

A forge has been operated here since the 17th century, firstly by the Weller family until the early 20th century and then by the Stovells until a few years ago.

The village fire engine used to be kept in the building facing the doors of the forge. The appliance, operated by a volunteer crew, contained hoses and a hand-worked pump.

The *Dolphin Inn*, opposite the forge, was one of the last inns in the county to brew its own ale. The brewhouse which stood in what is now the car park obtained its water supply from a horse-operated pump in the yard. Beer and cider were made at the *Dolphin* until 1926.

205 BUILDER'S WORKSHOP
TQ 210 497 ■

When a new vicarage was built in 1881, a local builder, Daniel Debenham, took over the old vicarage in Church Street together with the adjacent yard. In 1897 a Reigate builder, J King,

205: Builder's Workshop, Betchworth
Photo: Chris Shepheard

acquired the yard and erected the large workshop known as 'The White House'. This building had been moved from Reigate and re-erected in its present position.

In about 1920 the yard was taken over by George Cummins and Son, a major local builder with headquarters on Pebblehill Road, now Cox's Plant Hire. Cummins built a lot of houses and other buildings in the area and, like many builders at the time, were also coffin makers and undertakers.

This typical carpenter's shop is still in use, recently for furniture making by a group which included the Viscount Linley.

206 BAKERY
TQ 210 497

No 4 Church Street was a bakery from the early 19th century until the mid 20th century. The bakehouse contained a large oven fired by faggots.

GREAT AND LITTLE BOOKHAM
207 STEAM CORN MILL
TQ 133 549   **LS II** ■

This slated brick and stone 3-storey corn mill with cast-iron window frames dating from

c.1830 remains on the east side of Church Road complete with its brick chimney and adjoining mill house (**LS II**). The mill has been converted for residential use. There are some mill stones in the garden.

208 OLD ATLAS WORKS
209 NEW ATLAS WORKS
TQ 125 551 TQ 128 556

In the early part of the 20th century Thomas Gillett opened an engineering works (Atlas Works) in Little Bookham Street. In 1913 the company became Gillett, Stephens.

In 1917 Waring, of Waring & Gillow, bought Merrylands Hotel, which had been built opposite the station in 1885, shortly after the arrival of the railway. He built a factory (New Atlas Works) in the grounds and used the hotel building a offices.

During World War I both the Old and New Atlas Works were used for the production of aeroplane parts and other war equipment. Afterwards Gillett, Stephens and Blackburne & Burney operated in the factories making proprietary engines for a number of light cars and motor cycles.

In 1927 a Cotton motor cycle with a Blackburne engine won the Isle of Man TT race. Engines were made here for the Bleriot 'Whippet' car made by Air Navigation and Engineering of Addlestone, and the engines for the French-designed Marlborough car manufactured in the United Kingdom by the shock absorber manufacturers T B Andre.

Government contracts were again undertaken during World War II.

Bookham Engineering Company was founded in 1947 and they took over the Old Atlas Works. Originally they overhauled tractors and stationary engines but later they concentrated on steelwork fabrication and wrought iron

207: Steam Mill, Bookham
Photo: Chris Shepheard

211: Charlwood Forge

Photo: Charlwood Motor Co

work. After twenty years the firm moved to Kingston Road, Leatherhead. The Bookham factory was demolished in 1968 and flats named 'The Blackburn' now occupy the site.

Shortly after the war the factory opposite the station became known as 'Gillett Works' and was used by Wildt Mellor Bromley, a part of the Bentley Engineering Group. They manufactured hosiery-making machinery and hydraulic equipment, including undercarriages for Hawker aircraft. This operation ceased around 1980.

After this, the old hotel building was demolished and a new office built in its place for Photo-Me International. The 1917 factory survives and it is now used for the manufacture and servicing of self-operating photo booths for use world-wide.

CAPEL
210 BEARE GREEN FORGE
TQ 178 428   ∎

The forge at Beare Green was at the southern end of the village by the pond. It has now been converted to a private residence but externally the building is very little changed.

CHARLWOOD
211 FORGE
TQ 243 411   ∎

A forge has existed here since the 17thcentury; shoeing was carried out until the 1960s and other metalwork for about a further ten years.

Although the 17th century Forge Cottage was demolished in 1975 the blacksmith's shop remains behind the Charlwood Motor Company in a dilapidated condition. It contains two hearths with their chimneys forming an arch

within the forge. The building has its ridge tiles fitted in an interesting manner in order to provide ventilation.

212 HOOKWOOD FORGE
TQ 266 413   ∎

Five generations of the Bray family have operated this business in Hockwood since 1852. The original forge was 100 yards east of the present site, to which it was moved in 1886.

The blacksmith's shop was then in what is now 'Ingleside Bungalow'. The present business operates from a workshop at the rear and concentrates on mower repairs and sand-blasting. The shoeing of horses ended in 1948.

DORKING
213 THE DORKING FOUNDRY
TQ 164 494

No 62 West Street is believed to have been the site of a blacksmith's shop from about 1550, and also the site of one of the oldest foundries for casting iron in Surrey. In 1847 James Bartlett bought the property where he had been operating a forge and foundry. By 1871 the business of brass and iron foundry and forge was operated by Fletcher & Puttock but in 1881 the foundry was leased to Stone & Turner who also had a shop in the High Street, on the site occupied by Sainsbury's in 1995.

In 1918 the foundry was leased by W L Bodman Ltd. who made agricultural, road making and road sweeping equipment. They became the Road Plant Company, moved to Vincent's Lane, and were subsequently taken **49**

213: Drain Cover, Dorking   *Drawing: Peter Watkins*

over by Johnston Engineering Ltd. who still make road sweeping and similar equipment in Curtis Road.

The foundry was bought by Harold Carter in 1939. He carried out general iron casting as well as the manufacture of tile making machinery for Redhill Tile Company. In 1945 Redhill Tile Company set up a subsidiary company, Carter Wilkinson, to develop the engineering side of the business and particularly the manufacture of tile making machinery. At that time Mr Carter became a full-time working director of what was to become Redland and he engaged Richard Murdock to run the Dorking operation. The foundry was then known as Carter and Murdock for a number of years before it reverted to its original name of Dorking Foundry Ltd.

During World War II the machine shop was rebuilt, additional machine tools were installed and a large number of machine tools and munitions were produced, including 30,000 cast toilet roll holders. Up to 80 people were employed at this time.

Actual foundry work stopped in 1947 but throughout the Dorking area one may see cast-iron manhole covers, bollards, drain covers and other street furniture made at the Dorking Foundry.

In 1950 the front shop was again used as an ironmongers by Stone & Turner but this closed in 1969 when their business was taken over by Robert Dyas.

The Dorking Foundry continued to make machine tools. They also moved into the manufacture of armature winding machines for model locomotives and then wire bending and wire winding machines for making products such as chainlink fencing, transformer windings

and dartboards. The foundry left West Street around 1976 and moved to new premises in Curtis Road which eventually closed in 1992.

Around 1960 plastic model kits named 'Vulcan' and 'Eagle' were made on part of the West Street site by a Mr Asser.

In 1974 two of the former foundry buildings in West Street were leased by the Dorking Urban District Council to the Dorking and Leith Hill District Preservation Society for use as a museum which opened in 1976. Dorking and District Museum still operates in the foundry buildings, where it has a number of displays and documents relevant to the industrial history of the area.

214 COACH BUILDERS
TQ 168 497   ❖

Walker's coach building works were situated on the north side of the High Street in the late 19th century. In 1898 the weather-boarded workshop was demolished and replaced by a brick building with a terracotta frontage. This still stands and 'Pizza Express' at no 235 is at the original entrance to the showroom.

By 1882 the business was taken over by Ventham and Sons of Leatherhead, and from about 1920 it became a motor engineer's works, first occupied by Warne & Williams and then by Williams Motor Engineers. By the 1930s it had been converted into retail shops.

215-216 MALTINGS
TQ 163 494   ❖
TQ 164 494   ❖

Two old malt houses still exist in Dorking town centre, one in North Steet and the other in West Street. Both are now used for the present main industry of Dorking – the antiques business.

The building in North Street has bricks by the door at the south end engraved **W Attlee, July 1854**.

217 ROPE WALK
TQ 168 476   ❖

Charles Upfold, ropemaker, lived at 4 Flint Hill and at the beginning of the 20th century he had a rope walk opposite the Windmill Inn where the stretch of land between the road and the hedge is used for car parking.

HEADLEY
218 HEADLEY FORGE
TQ 202 551   **LS II** ■

A forge has operated here for well over one hundred years. In the early part of the 20th century there were up to five blacksmiths

218: Headley Forge   *Photo: Chris Shepheard*

220: Fire and Iron Gallery, Rowhurst Forge
Photo: Chris Shepheard

employed here. A blacksmith's and farrier's business is still carried on in the premises.

THE HOLMWOODS
219 WALKING STICK FACTORY
TQ 167 461

Henry Isemonger ran a walking stick factory just west of the A24 near the Norfolk Garage. The owner lived in a house by the factory which was called 'Promised Land' (now Solway House) in the garden of which was the Promised Land Chapel of which Mr Isemonger was the minister.

The factory operated from the early 20th century and was run in its later years by Mrs Isemonger until it closed in 1942. The firm supplied walking sticks and umbrella handles, both in the rough state to other makers or as finished articles for supplying retailers at home and abroad.

Wood shavings from the factory were put into the pond beside the *Norfolk Arms Hotel* and when the pond had been filled the Norfolk Garage was built on the site.

LEATHERHEAD
220 ROWHURST FORGE
TQ 160 586   ❑

This business was started in the 1930s, Rowhurst Forge being established after World War II. Richard Quinnell, who operates the company, has been a prime mover in the revival of the blacksmith's art in recent years, and is a consultant on the design, construction and restoration of ornamental metalwork. The company works mainly in iron but also in steel, bronze, brass, stainless steel and aluminium.

Their work is mainly ornamental; recent restorations include gates, screens and railings from Clandon Park, St Paul's Cathedral, Liverpool Cathedral and Ascot racecourse. Quinell's have produced ironwork for the restoration of Hampton Court and Uppark and

for remedial work on the Albert Memorial. A notable example of their work in the county is the Edward and Eleanor aluminium sundial in Tunsgate, Guildford.

221 COACH BUILDERS, BRIDGE STREET
TQ 164 564

Charles Ventham established a coach building business in Bridge Street in 1835 with a reputation for quality horse-drawn carriages. He was later joined by his sons Edward and Charles as the firm continued to make carriages and stage-coach type vehicles.

Later they produced bodywork for motor cars such as Daimler, Siddeley and Dennis; by the time of World War II they were describing themselves as coach-builders and motor engineers. They carried out a wide range of general engineering until Edward Ventham, the grandson of the founder, closed the business in 1936. By 1950 the works had been taken over by Motor and Air Products, plastic fabricators. Before the building was demolished in 1986 and replaced by an office block called 'The Coach House', an interesting petrol pump was removed and put on display at Leatherhead Museum. This is a Six-in-One

221/280: Theo Six-in-One Petrol Pump, Leatherhead
Photo: Chris Shepheard **51**

Multiple pump made by Theo & Co of Liverpool. The one pump was capable of being selected to supply petrol from six different tanks. The petrol was sucked into the pump from one of six storage tanks and then discharged into the vehicle by gravity.

Plans were made to incorporate a wheelwright's tyring platform in a paved area of 'The Coach House' but this did not take place.

222 B C U R A
TQ 162 571

The British Coal Utilisation Research Association (BCURA) was formed as a co-operative industrial research association in the government's grant-aid scheme. It was essentially a partnership between the producers of coal (represented by the Mining Association of Great Britain), the coal-burning appliance manufacturers and the coal users. The overall objectives were: improving efficiency in the use of coal, overcoming problems in existing applications caused by ash and sulphur and finding new uses for coal.

With the nationalisation of the coal industry in 1945 the National Coal Board (NCB) took over the coal producers's role.

The laboratories in Randall's Road were started in 1945, and by 1948 the operations from nine other sites were taking place there. Laboratory-scale activities included pioneering investigations into many uses of coal and coal-burning appliances together with pilot-scale activities into boiler and pressurised fluidised-bed combustion (PFBC).

By 1970 government grant-aid had ceased as did financial support from the NCB who already had their own (larger) research establishment. In 1971 the general research association activities ceased and part of the site was sold for property development.

The process department activities continued on the site as a self-financing entity of the NCB and carried out development work for a number of organisations world-wide until the middle of 1984, when activities on the site came to an end.

The PFBC equipment was dismantled and moved to the NCB research establishment near Cheltenham in 1986. The remaining buildings are in a neglected state.

223 P I R A
TQ 161 569　　　　　　　　　　　　　　■

The Paper and Allied Trades Research Association (PATRA) was established in 1929 and up to the time of World War II they had laboratories in London, in Shoe Lane and Charterhouse Street.

During the war many goods transported to forces overseas were arriving in an unusable condition and PATRA was asked to establish a packaging section. This operated in two converted houses in Acton.

After the war PATRA was another research association which was attracted to Leatherhead, opening its offices and laboratories in Randall's Road in 1948.

New packaging and engineering laboratories were added in the next few years until in 1967 PATRA merged with the Paper and Board Research Association of Kenley to become the Paper and Board Printing Industries Research Association (PIRA). All PIRA activities were transferred to Leatherhead after new paper and board laboratories were built in 1971, and the Kenley operation then closed.

224 C E R L, KELVIN AVENUE
TQ 157 575　　　　　　　　　　　　　　■

The Central Electricity Board, which operated the National Grid, had a small laboratory at Croydon substation to investigate insulator breakdown on the 132kV grid system. During air raids in World War II it was decided to move this department of one or two people to a hut erected next to the grid substation in Randalls Farm Lane, Leatherhead. The hut was superseded by a new building erected on the site in 1947-8, following nationalisation and incorporation of the transmission function with generation in the new British Electricity Authority. Thus the scope of the research activities of the British Electricity Research Laboratories was very much widened.

In 1958 the Central Electricity Generating Board was formed and a massive increase in research effort came about. At Leatherhead the old laboratories were retained to house the Materials Division only and the new CERL building in Cleeve Road was opened in 1961. employing over 750 staff.

At the lower end of the site, by the Rye Brook, a new high voltage testing laboratory was built in 1962. This remains as the research and development department of the National Grid

224: CERL Test Line, Leatherhead

Photo: Chris Shepheard

Company. However on privatisation, the main laboratory became vested in National Power, which closed down the rest of the site and transferred its research and technology activities to Swindon.

From the high voltage laboratory a test line extends to Oaklawn Road by Dorincourt. In the field alongside Randall's Road there was a linesmen's training school where activities included the erection and dismantling of overhead line towers as well as conductor stringing. The foundations and stubs of these towers still remain.

Thus, what started as purely a transmission research operation in 1940 and became a large multi-disciplinary research laboratory for the whole electricity supply industry, is again confining its activities to research and development for the transmission system.

225 LEATHERHEAD FOOD RESEARCH ASSOCIATION

TQ 161 570 ■

Another research associatio, the British Food Manufacturing Industries Research Association (BFMIRA), moved to Randall's Way, Leatherhead, in 1950. It was formed by the amalgamation of two earlier food research associations which had operated in Holloway since the 1920s.

Research is carried out into all types of manufactured foods and ingredients (except flour milling and baking and vegetable canning which are the concern of other organisations) and provides an information service for its members.

226 ASHE LABORATORIES

TQ 165 570

The chemical manufacturer A H Young & Sons was founded in London in 1936. The name was changed to Ashe Laboratories in order both to give a more scientific image and to move the firm's entry from the end of trade directories.

In 1947 they moved to Leatherhead, where they made Bandbox shampoo, Amplex tablets, Sucron, Lemskin and numerous other chemical products. Following a number of mergers their operations were transferred elsewhere and their Ashetree Works in Kingston Road was demolished and replaced by the Phoenix House office block.

227-228 ERMYN WAY, GOBLIN WORKS

TQ 183 566 ■
TQ 181 567 ■

From 1926 artificial silk (from one or two tons per day) was made here for a number of years by the Rayon Manufacturing Company; the operation closed due to a number of problems. Firstly, the process required large quantities of water and although boreholes were dug which produced over 1000 gallons per hour, this was inadequate. Secondly, the process produced unpleasant odours which caused considerable complaints from nearby residents.

Goblin (BVC) then moved on to the site to manufacture vacuum cleaners and other electrical products. The vacuum cleaner had been invented by H Cecil Booth, whose work included the design of engines for battleships and ferris wheels and supervision of the erection of the Connel Ferry Bridge in Scotland. Booth designed and patented the prototype in 1901, forming the Vacuum Cleaner Company Ltd [later to become Goblin (BVC) Ltd] a year later. The first machines were very bulky and were carried on a horse-drawn truck. This was parked outside the premises which were being cleaned and hoses were taken into the building to suck the dirt into a container in the van, using an engine-driven vacuum pump.

The first portable cleaner, made in 1904, was operated by two people, one to pump the bellows and one to use the cleaning tool. Electrically-driven portable cleaners were made from 1911.

In 1938 the company moved from London to the 22 acre site on the Ashtead-Leatherhead boundary where they were employed during World War II in making munitions such as fuses and igniters for shells, clocks for mines, breech blocks and firing mechanisms as well as

53

recording instruments for testing torpedoes and other equipment.

After the war there were around 1,000 people working on the site making portable vacuum cleaners and large fixed vacuumation plants for hospitals, ocean liners, power stations and major buildings including the Palace of Westminster.

By the end of the 1970s much of the property was around fifty years old and in need of replacement. The company had plans for rebuilding the plant in stages from 1982 to 1987 in a modern factory. By now the company was part of the international BSR Group and they sold the site and transferred their activities to Hampshire.

The factory was demolished in 1984 and in 1990 the new headquarters of Esso was opened on the site.

Just west of the Esso offices is the Remploy factory, adjacent to which is Milner House. The latter was a 19th century private house, The Long House, which was bought by the Ex-Services Welfare Society for the Mentally Disabled after World War I. Next to the house they built Hunter's Workshops as a sheltered workshop for the residents of the home.

Later the works was taken over by Thermega Ltd who were engaged in the manufacture of woollen goods, electric blankets and medical heating pads. They continued to employ disabled people from Milner House who made up about 25% of the workforce, In 1981 Remploy took over the factory and employ about 100 people of whom over 90% are registered disabled. The Manufacturing Services Group, of which Leatherhead Works is a part, operates as a contract manufacturer engaged in the batch production of electro-mechanical and electronic equipment, as well as the assembly of a wide range of products. Milner House is now a private nursing home which has no connection with the factory.

229-230 RONSONS
TQ 153 585
TQ 161 567

In 1918 Louis V Aronson patented the action for a cigarette lighter in the USA and by 1927 he had made the first single-action pocket lighter with the trade name 'Ronson'.

J Liddiatt imported and serviced Ronson lighters from premises in Grays Inn Road, an operation which transferred to Leatherhead in 1939.

They occupied Dorincourt in Oaklawn Road, a house built in the early part of the 20th century which had been unoccupied for about five years.

During World War II the company obtained government contracts to make incendiary bomb fuses, bomber gearbox parts, tension rods for aircraft and parts for guns. This enabled them to obtain machine tools and build workshops in the grounds of Dorincourt, employing several hundred people. During the war they bought Dorincourt as well as an 8-acre site in Randalls Road.

Towards the end of the war they tooled-up to make lighters under licence from Ronson Corporation (US) and the staff skills and the machine tools from their wartime work enabled them to convert easily to lighter manufacture. Production continued at Dorincourt until Ronsons opened their new factory in Randalls Road in 1952, selling Dorincourt to Queen Elizabeth's Foundation for the Disabled (see site 236-8).

The new factory continued to produce large numbers of cigarette lighters, the fuel gradually changing from petrol to butane. After some years with the US parent company in difficulties, and the UK subsidiary being instructed to market cheaper Japanese produced lighters, the factory closed in 1981 and was subsequently demolished to make way for a business park.

231 SPORTS CAR MANUFACTURE
TQ 164 567

From 1936 to 1959 Sydney Allard built nearly 2,000 hand-made sports cars at his south London factories, first at Putney and then, after World War II, at Clapham. From 1948 he opened an experimental workshop at Thorne's Garage (now Page Ford) in Kingston Road for a short time. The 'J' series of Allard cars which were later made in Toronto, were developed here.

232 SILK MANUFACTURE
TQ 182 557

At Wildernesse House at the entrance to Tyrrells Wood Lady Zoe Hart-Dyke began sericulture in 1932. She purchased 5,000 silk worm eggs which hatched and spun their cocoons, which she then heated in her domestic oven enabling the threads to be wound upon hand reelers. As the operation grew, a larger reeling machine was installed in the Hart-Dyke's garage and the local baker's oven was used for warming the cocoons in order to kill them.

Needing to expand, the Hart-Dykes opened a small factory in The Warren but were forced to close this due to complaints about the unpleasant smell. They then moved the operation to their ancestral home at Lullingstone in Kent.

233 CABLE MAKING
TQ 164 570

The General Cable Manufacturing Company was one of the largest employers in Leatherhead. They opened their works in Kingston Road in the 1930s and remained there until about 1969 when the works was closed and the buildings were demolished to make way for a business park.

Before the cable works was built the site was used as a brickworks and by a sawyer.

234 COACH BUILDERS
TQ 165 571

Karn Brothers were coachbuilders and blacksmiths on the corner of Kingston Road and Kingslea from the early 20th century. By the 1930s the site was occupied by a garage and remains so today.

235 TANNING
TQ 165 571

A tannery owned by Bartholomew and later Thomas Chitty operated from 1826 until the 1870s in the watermill upstream of the Town Bridge on the east bank of the river.

In 1888 one of the lead-lined baths was opened as a swimming pool and in 1900 this was taken over by St John's School until they built their own pool in the school grounds.

The area was cleared and the mill demolished after World War II for the construction of Minchin Close but traces of the watercourse may still be seen where it entered the river.

QUEEN ELIZABETH'S FOUNDATION FOR DISABLED PEOPLE
236 TQ 147 586 ■
237 TQ 153 585 ■
238 TQ 162 582 ■

Although this is a charitable organisation it is very much 'industrial', with most of its activities taking place in Leatherhead.

In 1933 Leatherhead Court, which had been a school for young ladies, became the Headquarters of what was then known as the Cripples' Training College (London and District) and a year later the first trainees were in residence. The college (later to become the Queen Elizabeth's Training College for the Disabled) undertook to train disabled men (women were not to come until 1950) for skilled employment in industry.

Once Ronsons had moved out of Dorincourt in Oaklawn Road (site 229) the college took over the house and factory and started to produce pottery and carry out assembly work, some of which was for Ronsons. Dorincourt developed sheltered employment facilities for printing and ceramic tile design and production which in 1994 expanded to a purpose-built factory at Bradmere House in Kingston Road (**TQ 162 582**).

Queen Elizabeth's Training College carries out welding, spray painting, electronic wiring and business studies. These operations both train disabled people for work elsewhere and employ disabled and able-bodied staff in both sheltered and normal factory conditions.

239-240 NEIL AND SPENCER
TQ 161 565
TQ 163 577

This company started making dry cleaning machinery in Clapham in 1937 before they were bombed and moved to the garage by Effingham cross-roads where they made aircraft components for the Ministry of Supply.

The firm moved to Leatherhead in 1947 and made dry cleaning machinery at their new factory in Station Road. By the 1960s the original works was too small for the output needed by what had become one of the largest manufacturers of dry cleaning machinery in the country. A second factory, Argosy Works, was therefore acquired in Kingston Road.

In 1963 the company moved into further production space in Redkiln Way, Horsham and by the late 1980s the operation had completely moved from Leatherhead.

LEIGH

241 FORGE
TQ 222 469 ■

This is one of many examples of a village blacksmith's shop becoming the local garage and petrol station. Old Forge Cottages are next door.

MICKLEHAM
242-243 FORGES, LONDON ROAD
TQ 173 540
TQ 173 537

There were two blacksmith's shops in the main London Road through Mickleham. With the construction of the by-pass and the increase in traffic both were converted to cafes.

The one at the northern end of the village was turned into 'The Old Forge Tea Room and Cafe' between the wars by its owner and it operated until the 1950s when it was demolished.

Further down, at the foot of Byttom Hill, the old blacksmith's shop became the 'Highway Cafe', now known as Frascati's.

244 BLACKSMITH, WESTHUMBLE
TQ 166 519

Lovedon Cottage (**LS 11**) was formerly a 17th century farmhouse called 'Birds and Abbotts' which was occupied by H J Baker from 1930 to 1960 when he used the outbuildings as a forge. Later his son ran a car repair business on the site.

NEWDIGATE
245 SCHERMULY PISTOL ROCKET APPARATUS
TQ 204 438

William Schermuly, an ex-sailor with an interest in life saving at sea, moved his company from Cheam to Mill Lane, Newdigate in 1933. Here they could manufacture their pyrotechnic distress equipment (flares, rockets etc) in the comparative safety of a remote and spacious site.

During the war the company expanded from their original 14 acre field until the buildings

248: Brook Cottages, Newdigate

Photo: Chris Shepheard

were spread over 55 acres and employed 1400 people. Gunpowder vans were often seen in Holmwood goods sidings, bringing in materials for the works.

In 1981 Schermuly's successors, Pains-Wessex, transferred what was by then a much smaller operation to Salisbury. By then only 140 people were working on the site.

A housing development is proposed for the original factory site.

246 FORGE
TQ 205 436

Gammages restaurant was built at the beginning of the century on the site of a blacksmith's shop. Behind this and 'Innstead' is thought to be the site of a gunpowder works in the 18th century.

247 NEWDIGATE FORGE
TQ 198 418 ■

As in many villages, the modern garage is on the site of a Blacksmith's forge. This one, and the one at Parkgate (site 246), were operated by the King family. This forge was run by William King from 1733 until the Overton family took over the business in 1870 and ran it until the end of the century.

248 CLOTHMAKING
TQ 200 428 ■

At the junction of Hogspudding Lane and Parkgate Road is Workhouse Green. This name derives from the fact that from about 1800 until the opening of the Union Workhouse in Dorking, following the 1834 change to the Poor Law, Brook Cottages were used to house the poor. In these cottages they carried out spinning and weaving to manufacture a heavy woollen cloth known as Newdigate Frizzle.

OCKLEY
249 BASKET MAKING
TQ 146 401 ■

Weaver's Pond on Ockley Green was used for over 100 years until 1912 for soaking withies for basket making. 'Weaver' Knight who carried out this work lived in a cottage beside the pond.

250 HOP DRYING
TQ 165 395 ■

One of the few oast houses in this part of the county forms part of the 17th century farm buildings at Stylehurst in Weare Street. The woodlands surrounding this farm were known as Old and New Hopgardens.

251-252 WHEELWRIGHT AND FORGE

TQ 148 404   **LS II** ■

TQ 148 401   **LS II** ■

Lime Tree Cottages, at the north-west side of the Green were built for the use of a wheelwright and a blacksmith, each having a workshop built on to the side of the house. However, from around 1830 both trades operated from a site just north of the Red Lion public house (*cf* Forge Cottages and The Forge).

253 HARNESS MAKER

TQ 147 402

Little Bookers was the workshop of a harness-maker and chandler, Penfold & Gibbs, which closed in 1965 after operating for well over 100 years.

WESTCOTT
254 FORGE

TQ 139 484

The business here was probably established in 1763, shortly before being taken over by the Ryde family who remained the owners until 1965.

Starting as a blacksmith, wheelwright and ironmonger, the firm took on cycle repairs just before World War I. Shortly after the war they undertook car repairs and petrol sales and this, like many forges, became the village garage.

The Ryde family continued to run the establishment until they sold the business and premises in 1965 to the Shell Petrol Company who demolished the buildings and replaced them with a modern service station.

In 1995 the service station is closed and the site is at present unused.

255 LAVENDER AND PEPPERMINT DISTILLING

TQ 150 484

From about 1893 lavender and peppermint were grown on farms around Westcott by Henry Chalke and James Kent. From the begin-

ning of the 20th century lavender growing was discontinued but peppermint was grown until 1914 or 1915. Milton Farm, Westcott Hill Farm, Florence Farm and Squires Farm had areas under lavender. Some was also grown near The Rookery.

At first the lavender and peppermint were sent to Mitcham for distilling but in 1898 a distillery was in operation at Westcott beside the Milton Brook at the end of Milton Street. In 1907 the Westcott farms were taken over by John Jakson & Co who in 1915 moved the distillery to their Croydon works.

255: Mint Distillery, Westcott
Kathleen Lane Collection

This chapter records a number of items of historical interest which have an industrial connection or which may not be described in other guide books. Again these are listed under parish or locality except for some items, such as Ice houses, grouped together for the District, from page 64 onwards.

ABINGER
256 CLOCK HOUSE
TQ 095 475   Clock only **LS II** ❖

The hammer clock at Abinger Hammer is one of the best-known landmarks in the area, reminding us of the connection between the village and the iron industry. The original clock on the site had no blacksmith and was moved to Abinger Hall stables (where it is still) in 1909 when the present clock with its striking smith was put in place.

257 ABINGER POUND
TQ 114 459   ■

The manorial pound which dates from the 17th century was where the lord of the manor held straying cattle. It still remains between the manor house and the church in what is now the garden of Abinger Manor Cottage, the former manor stables.

258-259 GRAVE MARKERS
TQ 114 459   ❖
TQ 110 444   ❖

The churchyard of St James, Abinger contains one or two wooden grave markers which are becoming comparatively rare. Also there is a cast-iron marker as well as a more modern one made of lead with the lettering formed from lead run on to the base plate.

Outside the churchyard are some punishment stocks (**LS II**) which are protected by a metal fence and a tiled canopy. The stocks were allegedly last used in the 1820s by the rector for boys who misbehaved in church.

In the churchyard of Holmbury St Mary there are at least six cast-iron grave markers, of which two are dated 1897 and 1910.

ASHTEAD
260-262 ORNAMENTAL GATES
TQ 190 581   **LS II** ❖
TQ 195 582   **LS II** ❖
TQ 192 589   **LS II** ❖

Elaborate wrought iron gates still stand at the entrance drives to Ashtead Park. The earlier ones at each end of Rookery Hill date from about 1800. A more ornate set carrying the date 1882 are by North Lodge in Epsom Road.

263: Buffer Depot   Photo: Chris Shepheard

BETCHWORTH
263 BUFFER DEPOT
TQ 211 510   ■

During World War II a number of 'buffer depots' were built throughout the country to hold strategic stocks of food and other supplies. During the Cold War period the depots were operated by private contractors for the government and contained food, cooking equipment, utensils, tents, tarpaulins etc. in case of a nuclear attack.

One such depot is number 339 at Station Road, Betchworth, which was operated by Butler's Wharf Ltd on behalf of the Ministry of Agriculture, Fisheries and Food (MAFF). It appears to be unused in 1995, but an application has been made for it to be demolished and houses built on the site.

262: Gates to Ashtead Park   Photo: Chris Shepheard

264: Staddle Stones, Bookham *Drawing: Peter Watkins*

BOOKHAM
264 CAST-IRON STADDLE STONES
TQ 133 547 ❖

The Old Barn Hall, on the west side of Church Road, Bookham, is built around a 16th century barn which was moved to its present position in 1906. Set in the front boundary wall of the property are 18 cast-iron staddle stones and it is assumed that the barn may have been standing on these before it was used as a hall.

The castings are marked **BARTLETT DORK-ING**. The Dorking foundry was established in the 1820s by the Bartlett family who operated there until 1870.

265 ORNAMENTAL DAIRY
TQ 140 550 **LS II** ■

Eastwick Park estate has now been developed for housing but a few estate buildings survive. Eastwick House was the Home Farmhouse; the cottages by Eastwick ponds were for game-keepers and the early 19th century dairy building survives in a private garden on the west side of Eastwick Drive.

Sale particulars of 1831 provide the following description: 'In a grove, on the skirt of the Park, and not far distant from the Dwelling are two small octagonal buildings Brick-built and Thatched; the one an Ornamental Dairy, the other a Scalding House, connected by a thatched open corridor'.

The thatched roofs have been replaced by decorative tiles; the buildings remain but are in need of some restoration.

BROCKHAM
266 POUND
TQ 198 495 **LS II** ❖

This brick-walled enclosure is in the north-east corner of the Green. The notice on the gate states that Brockham's own Act of Parliament of 1812 allowed only poultry to pasture on the Green. Cattle and horses were impounded until a fine had been paid to the Lord of the Manor.

CAPEL
267 FIRE INSURANCE MARK
TQ 176 407 ❖

On the cottage in The Street known as 'The Old Post Office' there is still a fire insurance plaque mounted on the front wall.

268 CAST-IRON GRAVE MARKERS
TQ 175 407 ❖

There are two cast-iron grave markers by the path from the lych-gate to the church. These were cast by Filmer & Mason of Guildford; one is dated 1880. There is also a marker made from iron strip.

CHARLWOOD
269 CAGE
TQ 243 411 **LS II** ❖

This cage or lock-up was used to house prisoners temporarily until they could be taken before magistrates in Reigate or Epsom.

It was the only building on the common and it is known to have been used in the 1790s. It is built of Charlwood Stone (see site 55) with brick quoins and with galletting between the stones. The cage had two small cells, with an

below: 265: Ornamental Dairy, Bookham
Photo: Chris Shepheard

271: Providence Chapel, Charlwood
Photo: Chris Shepheard

earth floor and iron bars at ceiling height to prevent escape through the roof.

In 1970 the building was restored and converted into an office used by the clerk to the parish council.

270 QUAKER CEMETERY
TQ 237 408 ■

In a field south of Tanyard Farm are some stone markers inscribed **FBG**. These indicate the area of the Friends' Burial Ground which existed here from 1661 to 1807, during which time 110 burials took place.

Edward Taylor left Tanyard Farm and adjacent lands to the Quakers in 1680.

271 PROVIDENCE CHAPEL
TQ 246 412   **LS II** ❑

This building was moved to Charlwood in 1816 having been part of Horsham Barracks. The barracks were built in about 6 weeks in 1796 to a standard pre-fabricated design; this is believed to have been the guard house.

This unique weather-boarded building with its verandah paved with Charlwood stone is still used as a place of worship.

DORKING
272 CAVES, SOUTH STREET
TQ 164 493 ❑

Dorking has a large number of man-made caves and underground passages. Most were dug to extract sand or to make cellars for storage. However, it is generally assumed that the South Street complex was constructed as a gentleman's folly. These are the only ones of any size which are accessible to the public. They are entered by a door beside the war

memorial and contain passages having a minimum width of 4 feet and a minimum height of 6 feet. There are a few hundred feet of passages, stairways and chambers in this underground complex.

From the early part of the 20th century the caves were used by various local brewers and wine merchants for the storage of liquor. In 1912 they were bought by Dorking Urban District Council whilst they were still being used for food and drink storage; the last such use was by H G Kingham and Co who left in the 1960s when their wholesale grocery business in Station Road closed.

Access may be gained by application to the Local History Group of the Dorking and District Preservation Society.

Further details may be found in *The South Street Caves Dorking* by Cliff Weight (1988). Other underground chambers in Dorking have been examined at the following locations:-

1 At the rear of the Strict Baptist Chapel behind 298, High Street

2 Under a house in South Street

3 Adjacent to Castle Mill

4 Under 157, High Street

5 Under 5, High Street. Once the *King's Head Inn* but later the magistrates' court. It has been suggested that the underground chamber may have been a cell for prisoners.

6 Under 37/39, High Street. This was the *Wheatsheaf Inn* and part of the underground construction was a cockpit, later used as a rifle range.

7 Beneath 94/98, High Street

8 Under 125/127, High Street. This was the *Sun Inn* until 1971.

9 Alongside 11, Rose Hill where the bricked-up access doorway may be seen.

Underground passages also exist in what were the grounds of Deepdene House (**TQ 173 491** ■). The house was used during World War II as the headquarters of the Southern Railway where over 500 railway staff worked. The two tunnels were extended up to 100 feet into the hillside and used as a telephone exchange, air raid shelter and control office.

273 STREET FURNITURE
TQ 16 49   Some **LS II** ❖

Dorking town centre is remarkable for the amount of street furniture it contains. As well as the pump and guide post at Pump Corner a large number of bollards and rails exist around the town. Many bollards were installed by the Dorking District Local Board (embossed **DDLB**) with later ones by Dorking Urban District Council (embossed **DUDC**) which was formed in 1895 to administer the same area.

Examples of these cast-iron bollards may be found in Horsham Road, South Street, Station Road, Chart Lane, High Street and alleys and paths in the vicinity. Of the 200 plus bollards some have various embossings, for example, a lady's leg and thigh, a key, a founder's name. Some were designed as lamp columns or fire hydrants.

With renovation to the paving around the town the use of cast-iron bollards is continuing. Some of the new pieces are embossed 'Dorothea'.

At the north end of Vincent's Lane lengths of railway line are used to support handrails, whereas wooden posts appear in Church Street.

Dorking also has a number of old sewer vent pipes, sometimes known as 'Wimbledon Columns'. As well as their primary purpose the columns also supported gas street lamps. Although the lighting fittings have disappeared, some columns may be seen in Rose Hill (2) and Roman Road.

274 FIRE INSURANCE MARK
TQ 168 493   ❖

Mounted on the front wall of 'Timber Hatch' in Dene Street there is still a fire mark issued by the Sun Insurance Company.

275 SONDES PLACE FARM
TQ 158 492   ■

This 19th century model farm, originally part of

276: Portland Road, Dorking   *Drawing: Peter Watkins*

the Denbies estate, was last used for farm buildings in 1921. The brick and flint buildings are built in the form of a rectangle with an arched gatehouse featuring a bell cupola and weathervane. The stables, cattle pens, barn and house were converted in 1986 to sheltered housing units.

In 1989 the development was given two awards: the Royal Institute of Chartered Surveyors and *Times* Conservation Award and the Regional Housing Design Award. The whole complex is an innovative re-use of the original buildings with minimum changes to the exterior appearance.

276 PORTLAND ROAD
TQ 163 496   ❖

This road is unique in that the houses are identified by letters rather than numbers. The letters are a permanent feature as they are set in the brickwork on the front of each house.

HEADLEY
277 GRAVE MARKERS
TQ 205 548   ❖

In Headley churchyard there are three cast-iron grave markers. These were all made at Dorking Foundry.

HOLMWOOD
278 GRAVE MARKERS
TQ 172 448   ❖

There are two decorative cast-iron markers in South Holmwood churchyard. They are dated 1884 and 1896 or 1886 and are in memory of Charles and Amey Worsfold. They are cast in the shape of gravestones with back plates fitted to them.

279: Corn Chandlery, Leatherhead
Photo: Chris Shepheard

LEATHERHEAD
279 CORN CHANDLERY
TQ 166 562 ■

Hutchinsons moved into their Church Street premises in 1830. Although the building was improved in 1870, many of the original features remain such as malting vats, malt cellar and stables. The firm continued as corn and coal merchants until 1965 when they dropped the agricultural side of the business and concentrated on the sale of fuel, fire irons, coal scuttles and decorative brass ware. The business is now known as 'By the Fire'.

280 HAMPTON COTTAGE, CHURCH STREET
TQ 167 562 **LS II** ☐

This 17th century cottage now houses the Leatherhead Museum of Local History. Its collection includes a gravity petrol pump from the coachbuilders in Bridge Street, some

62 278: Grave Marker, South Holmwood
See previous page
Drawing: Peter Watkins

281: Sewer Vent Pipe, Leatherhead
Drawing: Peter Watkins

cast-iron direction plates and a tyring platform from a forge in Bookham. There are also displays about the local firms of Ronsons, Goblins and the Ashtead Potters.

Towards the end of the 19th century Hampton Cottage and the adjacent Devonshire Cottage were owned by Albert Ockenden, and a photograph taken in 1895 shows a board above the window reading *Duke and Ockenden Ltd, Littlehampton. Abyssinian and Artesian Tube Well Sinkers, Tar Paving and Asphalte Layers etc. Established 1868.*

The Ockenden family, who were one of the leading suppliers of well equipment and pumps, continued to use Hampton Cottage as an office until 1909. The installation referred to site 156 was by Duke and Ockenden.

281 SEWAGE GAS VENT PIPES ❖

A number of tall cast-iron sewer vent pipes exist in Leatherhead and the surrounding villages. Examples of these apparently ill-maintained columns may be seen, among other places, at:-

TQ 176 569 Epsom Road, Leatherhead
TQ 186 577 Dene Road, Ashtead
TQ 191 582 Rookery Drive, Ashtead

TQ 193 591 Farm Lane, Ashtead
TQ 172 586 Links Road, Ashtead
TQ 174 575 Harriot's Lane, Ashtead
TQ 157 561 Cobham Road, Fetcham
TQ 146 555 Lower Road, Fetcham
TQ 135 546 Lower Road, Bookham
TQ 139 537 Dorking Road, Bookham
TQ 131 555 Church Road, Bookham
TQ 141 551 Lower Road, Bookham
TQ 134 545 Townshott Close, Bookham
TQ 175 556 Yarm Way, Leatherhead (2)
TQ 177 556 Reigate Road, Leatherhead

However a particularly ornate series exists, each of which has a spiral embossed decoration near the base and an elaborately decorated cast section below the slotted outlet at the top. Examples of these may be seen at:-

TQ 166 567 Linden Road, Leatherhead

TQ 179 586 Barnett Wood Lane, Ashtead, opposite *The Woodman* PH

TQ 164 567 Kingston Road, Leatherhead, opposite Randall's Road

TQ 163 578 Kingston Road, Leatherhead, corner of Aperdele Road

TQ 167 558 Dorking Road, Leatherhead, corner of Downs Lane

MICKLEHAM
282 ST MICHAEL'S CHAPEL
TQ 166 519   **LS II** ☐

The barn for 'Birds and Abbotts' farm was situated adjacent to where a cutting was being made for the railway and the bridge was being built near Westhumble station in 1867. A local resident, Elizabeth Vulliamy, obtained permission from the owner, Thomas Grissell of Norbury Park, to use the barn as a rest room and social centre for the navvies constructing the railway. In addition to organising Sunday services she wrote letters for the men and taught them to read and write.

When the railway construction was finished she continued to use the barn as a mission hall for Sunday services and, following a number of improvements, the building was consecrated and licensed as a chapel-of-ease to the parish church in 1904.

So the coming of the railway through Norbury Park in 1867 saved a derelict barn and gave Westhumble a church.

283 'THE STEPPING STONES' PUBLIC HOUSE
TQ 168 517

The original industrial part of Westhumble

282: St Michael's Chapel, Mickleham
Photo: Chris Shepheard

village, off Chapel Lane, had contained a sawyer's, carpenter's, wheelwright's, and undertaker's workshops and a builder's yard. At the time of the coming of the railway the nearest inn was the *Fox and Hounds* (now the *Burford Bridge Hotel*).

With all the additional visitors coming by rail the *Railway Arms* was built around 1870 on the site of the old craft workshops. The public house has been called *The Stepping Stones* since the 1950s.

284 HOME FARM, WESTHUMBLE
TQ 166 517   ■

In 1923 Victor Freeman bought Camilla Lacey, became the Lord of the Manor, and carried out a number of improvements to the village. One of these was the building of Home Farm, a model farm south of Chapel Lane. The farm buildings in a Dutch style were arranged in three sides round a courtyard with a pump in the centre.

The white weather-boarded farm buildings with a central clock tower together with workers'

284: Home Farm, Westhumble   *Photo: C Shepheard* **63**

cottages at each end and the pump under its tiled canopy remain in Pilgrim's Way. They are all now converted into residential properties: 'Barn End', 'The Byre', 'The Shippen', 'Stable Door', 'The Haybarn'.

285 PORTE-COCHERE
TQ 172 527   **LS II** ■

A very elaborate large cast-iron porte-cochere dating from c.1876 is at the main entrance to Juniper Hall.

286 SWISS COTTAGE
TQ 177 512   ■

John Logie Baird, the inventor of television, lived at Swiss Cottage on the top of Box Hill from 1929-1932. Whilst there, he conducted experiments from the house towards the town with light-finding equipment intended to assist aerial navigation in bad weather.

NEWDIGATE
287 SMALLHOLDINGS
TQ 215 417

The Small Holders Association bought the Cudworth Estate in 1902 and divided it into small plots on which the buyer could build one dwelling. The socialist slogan 'a few acres and a cow' gives the principle on which the development was based.

One of the plots was bought by Charles Almond as the base for Newdigate Holiday Camp in 1910, thought to be the first of its kind in the country, where guests spent their holidays under canvas. This was where the house called 'Almonds' now stands, and the area of the camp now contains mobile homes.

288 THE OLD BAKEHOUSE
TQ 196 422

On the south of 'Wirmwood', which was for years the village stores, was the old bakehouse which operated until 1931. Adjacent to it was a shoemaker's workshop. These two buildings were dismantled in 1988 for re-erection and use at the Weald and Downland Museum at Singleton in Sussex.

OCKLEY
289 WEAVERS' COTTAGES
TQ 162 401   **LS II** ■

Three 16th century timber-framed cottages in Weare Street are now combined into one large house known as 'Weavers'. These are believed

290: Milk Churn Platform, Ockley

to be cottages of 'illegal' weavers sited in an isolated position in order to avoid excise regulations which controlled weaving.

290 MILK CHURN PLATFORM
TQ 155 381   ❖

A feature which until recently used to be found outside many farms is a platform for milk churns. Since the use of bulk tankers, these have disappeared from the scene but one remains in Weare Street at the entrance to Holbrook Farm.

291 GRAVE MARKER
TQ 157 406   ❖

A cast-iron grave marker remains in Ockley churchyard leaning against a gravestone. It has no marking.

WESTCOTT
292 POUND
TQ 141 486   **LS II** ❖

This walled enclosure is situated in Westcott Street outside a house called 'The Pound'.

293 RIFLE RANGES
TQ 125 494 TQ 125 493   ❖

The remains of rifle ranges and butts may be seen adjacent to the footpath around 'Pickett's Hole'. Ranges were first built here during World War I.

Other ranges were to the west of Landbarn Farm, further along the same path.

ICE HOUSES
During the 18th and 19th centuries most large private houses had ice houses in their grounds for the storage of ice. Originally ice would have been taken from nearby ponds and laid in the ice house

between layers of straw, a drain being provided at the bottom to take away water as the ice melted. As soon as there was a railway network to transport it from the docks, an increasing amount of ice was imported, particularly from Norway. This ice would have been used in ice houses rather that obtained from (often dirty) ponds. The trade stopped during World War I, and the amount imported after the war was much less due to the number of plants which had been built in Britain for making ice mechanically. By the 1920s many large houses had refrigerators operated by paraffin or electricity and so the ice houses fell into disuse.

Some examples are given of ice houses which remain in Mole Valley District:

294 ABINGER HALL
TQ 105 472   ■

This late 18th century brick-built ice house is on raised ground to the south of the site of Abinger Hall with an eastern facing entrance. The Hall, which was situated on the north side of the A25, was built in 1783. The ice house was probably constructed at the same time as a well and pumphouse, all south of the road.

295 ASHTEAD HOUSE
TQ 196 585   ■

An 18th century ice house with a stepped entrance and a 10ft diameter dome, stood in the grounds of Ashtead House close to a large pond, into which it drained. The land has since been divided into separate plots; the ice house, which has been seen in the past few years, would now be in the garden of The Pines.

296 BETCHWORTH, BROOME PARK
TQ 211 505   ■

This brick-built ice house is 100 yards north of the house near the site of an old pond. It is built into an earth mound under trees with the tunnel entrance facing north. Except for the missing doors the ice house appears to be complete, although the chamber was filled with rubbish when examined.

297 BETCHWORTH, MORE PLACE
TQ 215 499   ■

There is documentary evidence for an 18th century brick ice house which is set into an artificial mound and largely hidden under trees.

298 BOOKHAM GROVE
TQ 137 542   ❖

At the time of the death of Viscountess Downe in 1912, among the outbuildings listed was an ice house. Brickwork in the verge on the west of Dorking Road, opposite the Chrystie recreation ground, could be the remains of this building.

299 BOOKHAM, POLESDEN LACEY
TQ 138 523

The OS maps of 1894 and 1933 both show an ice house in Preserve Copse, but the only construction in that position appears to be a pond for game. The National Trust knows of no ice house existing on the property.

300 CHARLWOOD, THE GREENINGS
TQ 225 416   ■

This brick building is set into a bank in the garden of the house. The walls were restored and the brick domed roof with its 2 ft earth covering removed in the mid 1970s. The inner part is oval in plan (about 10ft by 6ft) with a 6ft long tunnel entrance. The height of the tunnel was just over its present height.

Many of the bricks have been burned on the inside wall and it has been suggested that the structure may have been used as a lime kiln, particularly as pieces of chalk have been found under the brick floor. It is described as an ice house in 19th century maps and in early 20th century sale particulars. Situated close to a pond.

301 DORKING, DEEPDENE
TQ 173 493   ■

The ice house for Deepdene House still exists in the grounds of Kuoni House. It was built to look like a small temple approached by a flight of steps. There is a chamber leading off the entrance passage to the egg-sectioned house.

302 FETCHAM PARK
TQ 150 555

This brick-built 19th century ice house was cement-rendered. The roof over the entrance steps had been demolished for some time but the rest of the structure, at least above ground, was demolished in 1994.

The ice house is on the edge of a small quarry south of Fetcham Church.

303 LEATHERHEAD, RANDALLS PARK
TQ 154 571

The ice house (probably early 19th century) for Randalls Park House remained for a number of years in the grounds of Randalls Park crematorium. However it was demolished a few years ago by the crematorium company who state that it was being used by young people for illicit drinking and drug taking.

307: Ice House, Ockley Court

Photo: Chris Shepheard

304 MICKLEHAM, CAMILLA LACEY
TQ 163 519 ∎

There is documentary evidence of a rectangular ice house 6ft by 4ft and 4ft 6in high at the home of the novelist Fanny Burney and her French émigré husband General D'Arblay. The ice house was built into an artificial mound which had been made to afford a view of the house at Norbury Park from the garden.

305 MICKLEHAM, NORBURY PARK
TQ 165 542

This is a rectangular structure with flint walls and natural chalk floor. It is set in the hillside by Icehouse Combe; its roof has fallen in.

306 MICKLEHAM, JUNIPER HALL
TQ 174 527 ∎

The 19th century ice house is built into a small slope in the grounds of Juniper Hall Field Centre. It has an entrance tunnel with a separate chamber leading off it.

307 OCKLEY COURT FARM
TQ 157 408   LSII ∎

This 18th century ice house is above ground in the yard of Ockley Court Farm. The entrance tunnel and the circular 12-15ft deep well with a brick domed vault are covered by tiled roofs. In

1994 and 1995 the building is undergoing restoration by architects interested in conservation techniques, under the auspices of the Society for the Protection of Ancient Buildings.

308 WESTCOTT, BURY HILL
TQ 150 484 ❖

The entrance to this may be seen as a brick-arched doorway in the steeply rising bank to the south of a footpath near Bury Hill House.

309 WESTCOTT, ROKEFIELD
TQ 137 490 ∎

A 19th century egg-shaped ice house about 10ft at its widest is recorded as being near the driveway to the house.

310 WESTCOTT, THE ROOKERY
TQ 131 479 ❖

An 19th century brick-built ice house may be seen between the bridleway and the upper pond.

311 WOTTON HOUSE
TQ 123 469 ❖

This is situated in the bank, close to where the footpath from Friday Street, which passes to the east of the ponds in Wotton House grounds, turns to the right just above the house.

ADMIRALTY TELEGRAPHS

Two types of Admiralty telegraph were used between London and Portsmouth, the shutter system from 1796 until 1816 and the semaphore system from 1822 until 1848. The semaphore system had no stations within the present Mole Valley District; details of this system will be found in SIHG guides to Elmbridge District and Guildford Borough.

The route for the earlier shutter system, designed by Rev Lord George Murray, did cross the district with stations at Cabbage Hill (312: TQ 166 603 ∎), now known as Telegraph Hill, and Blind Oak Gate on Netley Heath (313: TQ 100 491 ❖).

The shutter system closed down in 1816. The buildings, which were never intended to be permanent, were small wooden two-roomed shacks with the frame containing the six wooden shutters mounted on the roof. No features can be seen at either site.

CITY POSTS (COAL TAX POSTS)

In order to help cover the costs of rebuilding after the Great Fire of 1666 the Corporation of London was allowed to levy a charge on all coal entering London. Subsequently there were a number of acts defining the boundaries of the area for which duty was charged until finally in 1861 the London Coal and Wine Duties Continuance Act redefined the London District as the Metropolitan Police District.

Posts were set up to mark the boundary in accordance with this Act of Parliament of the 24th and 25th years of Queen Victoria's reign, chapter 42 of the Statute Book. The cast-iron posts bear the Corporation of London crest and the inscription **24 25 VIC CAP 42** and were originally placed wherever a road or track crossed the boundary. Different types of marker posts were often employed beside railways, canals and rivers. The iron posts were cast by Henry Grissell at the Regents Canal Ironworks, Eagle Wharf, Hoxton; they are 6ft high of which 3-4ft is above ground.

The duties continued to raise money for engineering projects in London until the formation of the London County Council and the passing of the London Coal Duties Abolition Act in 1889.

Examples of city posts may be seen near the boundary of Mole Valley District at the following locations:-

319: Coal Tax Post, Ashtead
Drawing: Peter Watkins

314 TQ 166 599 ❖ On the west side of Kingston Road, outside *The Star* PH
315 TQ 172 601 ❖ At the north edge of Ashtead Common, south of Rushett Farm
316 TQ 178 606 ❖ At the junction of the bridleway north of the Common with that leading to Ashtead Station. **LS II**
317 TQ 183 612 ❖ In the verge on the north side of Christ Church Road.
318 TQ 182 612 ❖ Near the entrance to Glanmire Farm, Christ Church Road
319 TQ 180 609 ❖ At the junction of the bridleway east of Newton Wood with that on the north of the common. **LS II**
320 TQ 193 597 ■ On the down side embankment of the railway where it crosses the Rye.
321 TQ 194 594 ❖ On the north side of Dorking Road, a few yards towards Epsom from Craddocks Avenue.
322 TQ 199 583 ❖ On the east side of Pleasure Pit Road just before its junction with Headley Road.
323 TQ 201 579 ❖ Beside a footpath between Headley Road and Farm Lane.
324 TQ 201 574 ❖ In the verge of Langley Vale Road, opposite Headley Road

These are all cast-iron posts, except no 320 by the railway, which is a stone obelisk about 14ft high with the City's coat of arms on the front. This is of the type placed beside railways under an act of 1851 which defined the area of taxation as that within 20 miles of the General Post Office. It is, therefore, assumed that this post was moved here from another site, possibly Betchworth, when the area was reduced to the Metropolitan Police District ten years later.

320: Coal Tax Obelisk, detail *Drawing: Peter Watkins*

329: Pavilion Cinema, Dorking | *Photo: Chris Shepheard*

PLACES OF ENTERTAINMENT
ASHTEAD
325 CHURH ROAD
TQ 179 584 ■

This hall was built by George Baker after he bought the brickfield around 1905. It was first used as a silent cinema but by 1911 it had been converted to a roller skating rink. It was occupied by a print company in 1994.

DORKING
326 EMBASSY CINEMA
TQ 169 497

The Embassy cinema was on the site of the car park of the council offices at Pippbrook in Reigate Road. The cinema, which seated 1290, was opened in 1938 as the Gaumont. When it closed as a cinema in 1973 it became a meeting place for Jehovah's Witnesses until it was demolished in 1983.

327 CINEMA ROYAL
TQ 166 494

Films were first shown in Dorking in 1910 in the building in Club Court, south of the High Street, now used by the Salvation Army. This cinema closed soon after World War I.

328 ROYAL ELECTRIC CINEMA
TQ 164 491

The Royal Electric Cinema opened in South Street in 1913. It later became the New Electric and then the Regent before closing in 1939. After having been used as a furniture warehouse and auction room the building was demolished.

329 PAVILION CINEMA
TQ 163 491

This opened in 1925 a little south of the Electric but showed only 'talkie' films. It operated until 1963 before being used as a store for theatrical properties and now as a home improvement retailers. At one time a recording studio operated in the back of the building.

330 PUBLIC HALL
TQ 162 493

The Public Hall in West Street operated as a cinema, the Playhouse, from 1919 to 1930. It only ever showed silent films.

The hall was designed by Charles Driver and built by a private company in 1871. It has been used for many purposes over the years such as a cinema, theatre, petty sessions and county courts and a boys' high school.

Part of the ground floor became the headquarters of the volunteer fire brigade in 1881, the brigade having been formed in South Street in 1870. The fire brigade became full-time in 1912 under Dorking Urban District Council and the fire appliances and ambulances remained housed in this building until the new fire station was built in North Holmwood in 1971.

The building was used in 1994 as the headquarters of the county library service.

In the 1890s part of the ground floor was occupied by T H Sherlock & Son as a showroom and workshop for their coach building business. They left here in the 1920s for other premises in the town from where they developed the funeral service which today operates in South Street.

330: Public Hall, Dorking   *Photo: Chris Shepheard*

331 DORKING HALLS
TQ 170 497 ❑

These halls in Reigate Road were built in 1931 by a private company who got into financial difficulties and sold out to Dorking Urban District Council in 1946. They are still run by the local authority.

LEATHERHEAD
332 VICTORIA HALL
TQ 166 564

The Victoria Hall was on the north of the High Street; a plaque recalls its use as a theatre. Films were shown here as early as 1899 but the hall was used for all kinds of functions including gymnastic classes and Methodist meetings. In 1940 a cinema, the Picture House, then St George's, operated here. In 1950 this became the Leatherhead Theatre, which it remained until the Thorndike Theatre opened in 1969. The building was demolished to construct the Swan Centre.

333 THORNDIKE THEATRE
TQ 166 563 ❑

This was built on the site of the Manor House which had been demolished in 1936 to make way for the Crescent cinema. The cinema was in turn pulled down to enable the Thorndike Theatre to be built on the site.

334: Leatherhead Institute   *Photo: Chris Shepheard*

334 LEATHERHEAD INSTITUTE
TQ 168 565 ❑

The Leatherhead Institute was endowed and built in 1892 by Abraham Dixon who lived in Cherkley Court. He was a wealthy industrialist who retired to Leatherhead from Birmingham. His object was to provide working people with refreshment, education and recreation, initially for a subscription of 2d per week. A variety of activities have taken place in the building over the years; the first film show in the town took place here in 1898.

Having become very run-down the building was completely refurbished and re-opened in 1987, since when it has continued to provide community facilities for the town.

POST AND TELEPHONE

Some examples are given of letter boxes of some age or particular interest within the District. These are listed in alphabetical order of parish or locality.

335 ABINGER, FRIDAY STREET
TQ 127 458 ❖

An Edward VII lamp letter box is built into the wall of Pond Cottages on the opposite side of the lane from the pond.

Lamp letter boxes, made by Andrew Handyside & Co, came into use after the introduction of street lighting. They were intended to be used, mounted on a lamp column, in country areas where the amount of mail is small. Occasionally, as here, where there was no need for a larger box, they were built into a wall. As the inscription indicates they are only intended for letters.

336 ABINGER HAMMER
POST OFFICE
TQ 096 474 ❖

Here there is a George V Ludlow letter box of the pre-1936 design.

Originally letter boxes at sub-post offices were provided by the sub-postmaster, and were usually made by a local carpenter. From 1912 the Post Office supplied the boxes and James Ludlow of Birmingham received the contract to supply these steel-faced wooden boxes. Until 1952 the boxes had the distinctive enamel plate bearing the royal cipher and the words **POST OFFICE LETTER BOX**. There is an internal door allowing access from the post office as well as from outside.

337 ASHTEAD, OVERDALE
TQ 181 591 ❖

During the brief reign of Edward VIII in 1936 a total of 271 letter boxes were manufactured; of these 161 were pillar boxes. A number of boxes have since been changed and only pillar boxes remain with the cipher; there are 100 or so left in service. There were originally two in this part of Ashtead, indicating the period of its development. The one in Craddocks Avenue was replaced by a modern box when the post office moved to a different position but the original type 'B' (small) box made by the Carron Co still stands in Overdale, just over the level crossing.

338 ASHTEAD, BARNETT WOOD LANE POST OFFICE
TQ 179 585 ❖

The pillar box outside this post office is an Edward VII box made by McDowall Steven & Co of Glasgow (later Allied Ironfounders). This would date from between 1904 (when the posting aperture was put in the door, and when this company first supplied pillar boxes) and 1910 when George V came to the throne.

339 BOOKHAM, COBHAM ROAD
TQ 132 579 ❖

Opposite Slyfield House there is a Victorian pillar box. This was the standard box from 1887 made by Andrew Handyside & Co. Before that date there was no royal cipher nor the words **POST OFFICE** on either side of the posting aperture.

340 DORKING, HORSHAM ROAD POST OFFICE
TQ 165 485 ❖

This sub-post office has a larger Ludlow box than that at Abinger Hammer and was installed during the reign of Edward VII. During the 1980s the enamel plate was forcibly removed from the box.

339: Victorian Pillar Box
Photo: Chris Shepheard

341 HEADLEY, CHURCH LANE
TQ 520 552 ❖

Mounted in the wall of Headley Park there is a Victorian wall box manufactured by W T Allen & Co between 1881 and 1904.

342 LEATHERHEAD, KINGSTON ROAD POST OFFICE
TQ 165 572 ❖

Outside this sub-post office is a Victorian type 'B' (small) pillar box made by Handyside. As this box has a royal cipher it dates from between 1887 and 1904.

343 LEATHERHEAD, KINGSTON ROAD
TQ 166 599 ❖

A Victorian wall letter box is built into the wall outside D'Abernon House on the east side of the road near the District boundary. This was manufactured by W T Allen & Co between 1881 and 1904.

344 MICKLEHAM, BYTTOM HILL
TQ 172 538 ❖

An Edward VII wall letter box by Allen is mounted in the flint wall at the bottom of Byttom Hill by Dorking Road.

345 WESTCOTT, MILTON STREET
TQ 148 487 ❖

A small Victorian wall letter box of the 1881 design is mounted with a concrete surround in the wall of Old Bury Hill Gardens.

TELEPHONE KIOSKS

Since the 1980s, British Telecommunications have been replacing the traditional red telephone kiosks with the modern vandal-proof type. Some of the earlier boxes, known as the K6 type and designed by Sir Giles Gilbert Scott in 1924, still exist. Some of these have been Listed, Grade II, including the following:

346 TQ 118 382 ❖ Abinger, Walliswood Green Road
347 TQ 197 494 ❖ at Brockham Post Office
348 TQ 164 492 ❖ Dorking, South Street
349 TQ 224 469 ❖ Leigh, Leigh Place Road
350 TQ 167 518 ❖ Westhumble, outside the Railway Station

DEFENCE OF THE REALM MOBILISATION CENTRES

Until Victorian times London, unlike other European capital cities, had no defensive ring of forts. This was because it had always been assumed that the Royal Navy could adequately protect our shores. In the late 1880s doubts arose about the ability of the Navy to give this protection and General Sir Edward Hamley produced a plan whereby the capital could be protected by the London Volunteers in the event of an invasion.

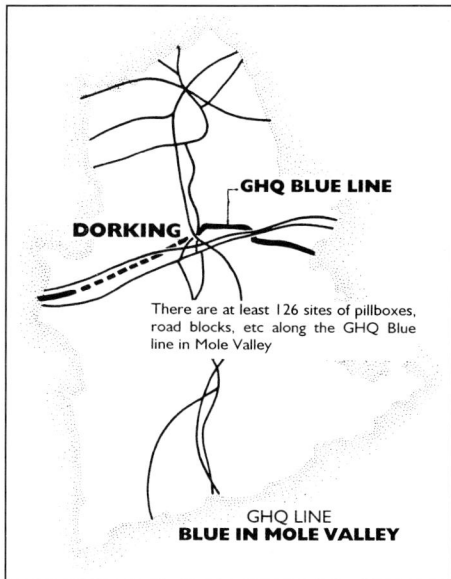

GHQ BLUE LINE

DORKING

There are at least 126 sites of pillboxes, road blocks, etc along the GHQ Blue line in Mole Valley

GHQ LINE
BLUE IN MOLE VALLEY

GHQ Line, Blue in Mole Valley

A line of 13 lightly-fortified mobilisation centres was built to store munitions, stores and trench-digging tools. In an emergency the Volunteers would have dug trench lines which would have been supported by the mobilisation centres or 'forts'.

The plan for this defensive system was approved by Parliament in 1889 but construction was slow until the impetus from the South African War caused the buildings to be completed in 1902. Three of these centres were in Mole Valley District.

351 DENBIES FORT
TQ 155 511

This was demolished in 1970 and there is nothing to be seen of the fort. It was abandoned by the government in 1905, then used as a private house, before being used as a grain store in the 1960s. The house, 'The Fort', which was the caretaker's cottage and store, remains.

352: Mobilisation Centre, Boxhill   *Photo: C Shepheard*

352 BOX HILL FORT
TQ 177 514   **AM** ❖

The site for this fort was purchased in 1891. The mobilisation centre was an infantry redoubt but it includes magazines for artillery ammunition to be used by batteries in nearby field emplacements.

In 1908 it was sold back to the original owners and in 1914 it was given to the National Trust who are in 1995 carrying out renovations to restore the fort building. The metal bullet-proof shutters and doors have been repaired and the roof has been made waterproof. An interpretation board gives details of the fort and the defensive system.

The National Trust information centre and shop are housed in what was the caretaker's house and store.

353 BETCHWORTH FORT
TQ 201 515   ■

Situated at the top of the Downs above Brockham Limeworks, access from Fort Road.

The fort, cottage and land were sold back to Deepdene Estates by the government around 1909 and the fort buildings were lived in at least from 1921, when Deepdene Estates sold the property, until 1983.

The caretaker's cottage has always been inhabited but the fort is now a store. The boundaries of the property were indicated by stone markers inscribed **WD** and some of these remain. The fort is similar to that at Box Hill, with metal shutters and doors still in place.

WORLD WAR II DEFENCES

During World War II the Mole Valley District played an important role in the defence plans for southern England. The country was crossed by a number of defence lines designed, under the direction of General Sir Edmund Ironside, to delay, if not stop, the enemy's approach from landing beaches and ports towards London. The entire scheme was virtually completed within the space of a few months in the summer of 1940, becoming operational once only, during the September of that year.

The principal stop line in the south was the GHQ Line Blue, stretching from the Bristol Channel to the Thames Estuary. The line entered Mole Valley on the scarp face of the North Downs at Hackhurst. Pillboxes continued eastwards towards Ranmore Common, the defences made use of the steep hillside. On Ranmore, a large military camp was established, with anti-aircraft guns. However, from here to Dorking there appear to be no pillboxes.

Dorking formed a major strong-point on the line, and the town was very heavily defended in order to protect the Dorking Gap which would have been a route to the capital. East of Dorking the line left the high ground and used the River Mole until it left the District near Wonham Mill to continue south of Reigate.

Particularly good examples of pillboxes are found at (**354**) TQ 113 487, which was convincingly disguised as a cafe; and at (**355**) TQ 193 503.

A large number of anti-tank blocks of various designs are to be found in the District, a group of 20 to 30 are on the railway embankment at (**356**) TQ 170 501.

A map of the World War II defence system for Dorking may be seen in Dorking Museum.

ACKNOWLEDGEMENTS

A large number of people have provided information for this book, or granted access to their properties so that features could be viewed. To all these I express my sincere thanks.

I would particularly like to acknowledge the help given by Glenys Crocker, Alan A Jackson, Derek Renn, Jean Shelley, Chris Shepheard and Peter Watkins.

Much information was willingly provided by the Planning Department of Mole Valley District Council; the libraries of Dorking Museum, Leatherhead and District Local History Society and the Surrey Archaeological Society. Some information on the gas and electricity industries was obtained from the Gas Museum and the Milne Museum respectively whilst the East Surrey Water Company and Thames Water Utilities provided historical details of the water industry. A number of other companies, or members of their staff, helped with historical information about their operations; to all these thanks are due.

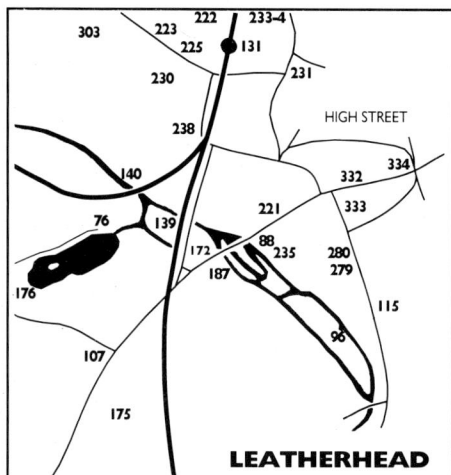

LEATHERHEAD

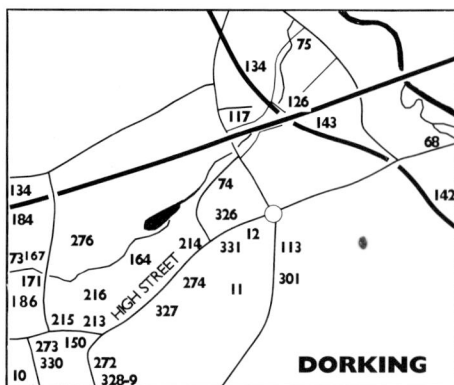

DORKING